The Case for Rage

The Case for Rage

*Why Anger Is Essential
to Anti-Racist Struggle*

Myisha Cherry

OXFORD

UNIVERSITY PRESS

Oxford University Press is a department of the University of Oxford. It furthers
the University's objective of excellence in research, scholarship, and education
by publishing worldwide. Oxford is a registered trade mark of Oxford University
Press in the UK and certain other countries.

Published in the United States of America by Oxford University Press
198 Madison Avenue, New York, NY 10016, United States of America.

© Oxford University Press 2021

CIP data is on file at Library of Congress

ISBN 978-0-19-755734-1

DOI: 10.1093/oso/9780197557341.001.0001

1 3 5 7 9 8 6 4 2

Printed by LSC communications, United States of America

In memory of
Thandeka Mdeliswa,
aka
Superstar.
You will always be loved
and never forgotten!

Contents

Preface

I write these words in the fall of 2020. The world is still in the grip of a global pandemic that began in early March of this year in the United States. In response to COVID-19, classes at the university where I teach immediately went online. I prepared myself as best I could for this new normal of academic life. The course I taught that spring was a social philosophy course, "Struggle and Protest." My students and I attempted to make sense of the nature of resistance and arguments for its justification, as well as the role of anger and hope in the face of what seems like perpetual struggle. I had never taught online before. Most of my students had never taken an online class. It was a new experience for us all. I was ever so conscious of the unique challenges my students, who are predominately people of color and first-generation college students, would have during this tough time. How could they focus on philosophical questions when they and people who looked like them were losing their jobs, falling ill, even dying—difficulties that data reveal were highly correlated with race.

The course, unfortunately, could not have been timelier. As our semester went on, anti-racist protests were occurring around the world in response to the police killings of Breonna Taylor in March and George Floyd in May. Video footage revealing the details of the killing of Ahmaud Arbery appeared in March. Two months earlier, white men chased him down and murdered him in a case of "jogging while Black." Witnesses reported that the shooter used a racial slur after the shooting, and the white men were authors of several racist posts on social media. Arbery's killers would have gotten away with murder if journalists didn't publicize the story. My students, of course, were angry.

During this time, more people began to take up the mantra of Black Lives Matter (BLM). This uptake was quite different from when Alicia Garza, cofounder of Black Lives Matter, originally expressed it online in response to the shooting of Trayvon Martin in 2012. This time it *appeared* that America was finally getting it. People publicly incited All Lives Matter retorts less and less. Businesses released online statements in support of Black folk. Institutions took up the challenge to become more diverse and inclusive. And allies in other countries marched in solidarity, as well as protested racism occurring on their own soil.

However, police shootings of Blacks continued. A white teenager was arrested for killing two Kenosha, Wisconsin, protestors. He was eventually released on $2 million bail, paid for by a pillow entrepreneur and a 1980s sitcom actor. Hate groups like the Proud Boys went public later in the year. A Republican legislator in New Hampshire told people on Facebook to burn and loot homes with BLM signs. A twenty-four-year-old white man was charged with ethnic intimidation in Michigan for shooting into a family's home because they had BLM signs in their window. *Racism can be quite resilient.*

British Nigerian actor John Boyega, known for his role in various *Star Wars* movies, used his platform to speak out against racial injustice. Speaking with pain *and* anger at a London rally organized to protest the shooting of George Floyd he said, "Look, I don't know if I'm going to have a career after this, but f— that. . . . Black lives have always mattered. . . . We have always been important. We have always meant something. We have always succeeded regardless. And now is the time. I ain't waiting. I ain't waiting."[1] In the summer, WNBA and NBA players, coaches, and owners also used their platforms to promote anti-racist messaging, freely expressing their emotions. When an officer shot Jacob Blake seven times in the back in August, the Los Angeles Clippers' owner wrote on Twitter, "I am again angry over the shooting of a Black man." When the Kentucky attorney general failed to indict officers on murder charges for the killing of Breonna Taylor, NBA star LeBron James noted how "devastated, hurt, sad, *and* mad" he was over it.[2]

The anger many were feeling was not just in response to the police. This was a rage that was boiling over from other racial incidents and injustices. It was directed at the forty-fifth president. During the president's election campaign and his presidency, he often expressed racist ideas (e.g., "When Mexico sends its people, they're not sending their best. . . . They're bringing rapists") and instituted policies that disproportionally impacted nonwhites (e.g., the Muslim ban). Their anger was also directed at fellow citizens. I had grown up watching historical footage of hate groups like the Ku Klux Klan. They may have expressed pride in being white, but their hoods signified shame. Not in this era! White nationalists and white supremacists got bold. They marched hoodless in Charlottesville, Virginia, to protest the removal of a statue of Robert E. Lee and chanted, "Jews will not replace us," in the streets. And the alt-right attempted to rehabilitate the public image of white nationalism. They had some success when the magazine *Mother Jones* described their leader, Richard Spencer, as a "dapper white nationalist."[3]

It's easy to blame a president, white nationalists, and white supremacists for America's racial problems. If only it stopped there. Thanks to technology, many began to share their own racial encounters. Through online videos and social media testimonies, we increasingly saw that people were constantly harassing Latinx folk for speaking Spanish and accusing them of being illegal, white women were calling the police on Blacks for no reason other than being Black, and only a few people seem to care about or were bringing mass attention to missing Indigenous women in the United States. W. E. B. Du Bois wrote in the second chapter of his seminal text *The Souls of Black Folk* that "the problem of the twentieth century is the problem of the color line."[4] We are twenty years into the twenty-first century and four years from when the first Black US president left office. Still this problem exists. This problem and America's unwillingness to address it have made many people angry—angry like never before.

Booker T. Washington, a figure whose work my students and I engaged with in the course, expressed to whites in his "Atlanta Compromise" speech that the formerly enslaved were "the most . . . unresentful people that the world has seen."[5] To say that Blacks are not a resentful people is to make an essentialist claim about how all Black people feel and who they are by the very fact of their Blackness. This kind of essentialism is false. However, while

Blacks as a group are not by their very natures a resentful people, this doesn't mean that today many Blacks and nonwhites (along with their white allies) do not have justifiable reasons to be angry at racism, *and* many are in fact angry. So what should Black people do with this anger? What should anyone do with anger at racism—the profound, justified rage that, not only after the events of 2020, but in the public and private sphere pre-2020, so many of us have felt and are still feeling?

In an essay for *The Atlantic* titled "Anger Can Build a Better World,"[6] as well as in interviews with BBC and Monocle Radio about the anger of Portland protestors, I said that anger has important communicative functions in an unjust world. It can remind us that the lives of the marginalized matter and make us aware of the fact that racial justice is lacking. It also motivates productive action toward creating a more just world. I received interesting responses from readers and listeners. Some agreed with me but suggested we should be cautious with anger. Others conceded the fact that anger at racism can be motivating, but they believed that "it is so often expressed as violence towards the innocent," and that "anger is not the great communicator. . . . We don't need that now."[7] This convinced me even more that there needs to be an elaborate case made for rage at racism. That's what you'll find in this book.

How can we make sense of this strong emotion we feel in response to racism's many forms and manifestations? Why are so many afraid of it? How can we better respond to others who are angry? Does anger have a role in anti-racist struggle and protest? The more we reflect on these questions, the better equipped we are to fight the good fight, or at least get out of the way of those who dare to step on the battlefield for racial justice.

Acknowledgments

Thinking and writing are never done alone. They take place in community. I am grateful for a community that has inspired and challenged my thinking on anger, provided space for me to write, and nourished my heart and mind when thinking became tiring and doubts began to creep in that this project would ever see the light of day.

Thanks to Lawrence Blum and Christopher Lewis for believing in me and the ideas in this book when they first appeared as a six-thousand-word writing sample for graduate school admissions. I will never forget your kindness and attention.

Lucy Randall, your belief in this book is one of the main reasons it exists. Your editorial support has helped me write a better book. Thank you. Special thanks to Hannah Doyle for making this process as smooth as ever.

This project would have taken longer to enter the world if it wasn't for the help of my research assistant, Chris McVey. We both experienced some struggles while preparing this book for publication. But his commitment to make it happen, despite it all, was and still is inspiring.

Academics have so much on their plates. So when they take time out to read your work and provide helpful feedback, it not only reveals how smart they are, more importantly, it tells you how selfless, thoughtful, and loving they are. Thanks to Chris Lebron, Kathryn Norlock, Alice MacLachlan, Owen Flanagan, Kim Frost, Brandon Terry, Nicolas Bommarito, and anonymous reviewers for your suggestions, pushback, and questions.

The ideas in this book benefited from audience engagement at conferences, colloquiums, and institutes. Thanks to the following institutions and departments for inviting me to share my work: University of Wisconsin–Madison, Claremont McKenna College, PIKSI Program at MIT and Penn State University, Wits University, Elon University, Cal State Bakersfield, CUNY Graduate Center, Cal State Los Angeles, UC Riverside, Buffalo State University, Stellenbosch University, UC San Diego, Brown University, Society of Philosophy and Psychology, Marquette University, Princeton University, Wesleyan University, University of Michigan at Ann Arbor, Harvard University, University of North Carolina at Charlotte, TEDx audience at University of Illinois, Chicago, and the House of Beautiful Business.

During my first semester at the University of California–Riverside I taught a graduate seminar on the moral psychology of anger. In the last week, students workshopped draft chapters of this manuscript with excitement, generosity, and rigor. It benefited tremendously as a result. Much thanks to Abel Ang, Jonathan Baker, Taylor Doran, Alba Cercas Curry, Kristen Ekstrom, Victor Guerra, Tommy Hanauer-Rehavia, Marie Evanston, Rotem Herrmann, Osup Kwon, Maxwell McCoy, Deborah Nelson, Micaela Quintana, David Shope, Jared Smith, Marek Twarzynski, and Katherine Vidueira.

Shout out to the various writing groups that provided space, community, and accountability. The Virtual Stanford writing group led by Wendy Salkin and the UCR women's writing group led by Kim Yi Dionne benefited me richly. To my writing partner, Luvell Anderson, I look forward to writing with you every week. Thanks for your energy, advice, and particularly your patience when I talk way beyond our allotted break time.

Special thanks to Axelle Karera and Kris Sealey for being my personal Black woman philosophers' support system. Your wisdom, empathy, strength, and humor helped me get through revisions after revisions. Because of you, I am inspired every day to #MEM.

To my department colleague and workout partner, Adam Harmer. You are a hell of a friend! Thank you for listening to me when I vent, reading my work although it has nothing to do with your early modern research area, and inspiring me to constantly stay strong and fit. When the going gets tough, you bring me smoothies, send me workout texts, willingly participate in my outdoor adventures, and so much more. (Let's continue to fall off bikes together on our road to tenure.)

Introduction

I'm sure that every African American can recall the first time they were called the N-Word. My first experience occurred when I was seven years old. I was playing with a white friend of mine outside of an apartment complex in Wilmington, Delaware. I don't remember his name. All I know is that we used to play together a lot and got along quite well. That was until, one autumn day after not seeing him for a while, I went up to him to say hello. He replied emphatically, "My daddy told me I can't play with N*ggers!"

I was hurt! And I was angry!

If seven-year-old me was ignorant of the word's meaning, I could have escaped the pain and the fury. If he would've hurled the words "ignoramus" or "deplorable" at me instead, I would have been too clueless to be insulted. But at seven, I knew what *that word* meant. It was not something you only ran across in big dictionaries, buried between words that began with the letters M and O. No! That word had a long history and it was a weapon that anyone could use against humans with Black skin, including children.

I *do not* remember my first kiss. I *do not* remember the first book I ever read.

I *do* remember the first time I was angry. And it was at racism.

I wish I could say that was the last time I was outraged and the last time I experienced racial mistreatment. As years went by, I realized that racism was a reality—often daily or every now and again if you were lucky. But my response to it would remain the same. Racism and the people who practiced it deserved my rage.

When my primary school teachers showed us calm responses to racism via *Eyes on the Prize* documentaries, which told the story of

Blacks' fight for civil rights in the United States, I was that student always boiling with rage at my desk as I watched whites brutalize African Americans in the Jim Crow South. I saw my own rage reflected back to me when I learned about people fighting slavery and racism in history. I read about angry responses to racism in the poetry of Black Arts Movement writers who were able to express it with rhythmic eloquence. I witnessed this rage as I watched live footage of the Los Angeles riots in 1992. While wrapping up my senior year in college, I wanted to escape to New York City to express my rage with other outraged folks when I heard that the New York Police Department had shot Amadou Diallo forty-one times—and had gotten away with it!

More recently, I've experienced anger at racism more and more. Racists have become much bolder and more shameless since the election of the forty-fifth president. I am not alone in noticing this. People come to me privately to help them make sense of their feelings. I know of outraged folks who have marched daily in response to the shootings of Black men and women at the hands of the police. From Baltimore to Portland, Ferguson, and Kenosha, people are angry at racism. And it's not just Blacks either. Folks with different hues of skin and regional accents, who are from different economic backgrounds and different countries, are mad as hell at racism and its normalization in the United States.

In response, some critics seem to think that what is most strange and alarming about this time is the angry reactions of anti-racists, and not the racism itself. Perhaps they think anger is the true threat to our democracy. In white supremacist societies, anti-racism has always been considered dangerous. In places that pride themselves on being rational, emotions have always been in the hot seat.[1] Combine these two contexts together and you have a culture that—instead of being rightfully challenged by such anger—is likely to view the emotions of anti-racists with suspicion and fear. And in such a culture, there are likely to be just as many anti-racists who are ashamed of their rage as there are those who embrace it.

* * *

Emotions help us grapple with the world. Some alert us to danger, aid in decision-making, and motivate our actions. Others help us understand ourselves and other people. And they assist us in tempering our actions.

For these reasons, Charles Darwin claimed that emotions are adaptations that help us survive and reproduce. Robert Solomon, a scholar who wrote extensively about emotions from a philosophical perspective, adds an existential outlook by noting that emotions are what allow us to have a meaningful life. He states, "It is because we are moved, because we feel, that life has a meaning."[2] However, Solomon does admit that the type of emotion matters; while all emotions make life meaningful, some meanings are demeaning. Love, for example, may enhance our life, while emotions like sadness may define our lives as pitiful.

Emotions are also social and political. They are directed at and engage the social and political world. Humanists remind us that all kinds of political societies are filled with people who have emotions that are directed at the nation-state, political principles or policies, and political citizens. These political emotions also play a role in our lives. They can reinforce oppression or motivate us to fight it; they can derail the pursuit of justice or expedite it; they can enliven us or make us politically apathetic. Some emotions are presumed to do a better job in the political sphere than others—or at least do the job with fewer moral risks.

Compassion motivates us to engage in altruistic action and create egalitarian institutions.[3] And many think that citizens must feel patriotic love in order for a political culture to survive and flourish. Only then are we able to focus on general welfare rather than our own selfish pursuits. Many think that *only* emotions like compassion and love can help us to engage in positive action in order to achieve these goals, whereas other emotions—less positive ones— are considered a threat.

We often tend to see "negative" emotions like fear and anxiety as barriers to liberal political goals. Fear can be a problem for democratic self-government since it can give rise to othering and scapegoating. Political scientists have described how public fears create public desires that often legitimize unfair policies. And these policies disproportionately affect certain racialized peoples. For example, fear of Blacks as "hyperviolent" impacted prison expansion. Anxiety over Latinos becoming the majority led to the legitimization of the US Immigration and Customs Enforcement (ICE). And fear of Arab men as violent and hyperpatriarchal was used after September 11, 2001, to create public fear of terrorists, support for war, and profiling and surveillance initiatives. Such racial politics of emotions reinforce oppression.[4]

But there is one political emotion that we tend to be *overly* concerned about. It's the emotion I felt at seven years old. It's the emotion many experienced when George Floyd's and Eric Garner's cries for help were ignored, when white supremacists were described as fine people by an acting president, when Sandra Bland never made it home, when members of a white militia killed anti-racist protestors in 2020, and when COVID-19 was downplayed by officials as the outbreak continued to have a disproportionate effect on communities of color. So many are worried about anger and doubtful about the positive role it can play, but it is plainly true: there is a lot to be angry about.

Anger is thought to cause disruption.[5] In her 2016 book *Anger and Forgiveness*, philosopher Martha Nussbaum claims that anger involves down-ranking the wrongdoer to a moral position that is beneath us and a desire for payback and revenge. Though it may have an evolutionary history—helping with our fight-or-flight response by serving as a signal, motivation, and deterrent—she doubts that it is necessary today. Although she admits that anger can be useful, this use is limited. It is useful until things go astray, and given what anger involves, it often does go astray.[6] Anger, in her view, is also an impediment to other emotions and attitudes that are needed to construct a better future, such as generosity, empathy, and love. Therefore, when she considers the role of anger in the context of political injustice she writes, "It is a bad strategy and a fatally flawed response."[7]

Owen Flanagan also doubts that anger is necessary even in cases in which it can work. In *Geography of Morals*, he considers a story retold by Nussbaum of a child who was rescued from a concentration camp by a soldier in the Allied forces. The soldier revealed to the child how angry he was about what the Nazis were doing in the camp. By doing so, the soldier helped the child recognize that the humanity that the Nazi oppressors had denied the prisoners in the camp still existed in the world—and would prevail. Rage was the sign that morality had returned. Flanagan questions if only anger could have served this purpose, however: "Suppose that instead of fury at the evidence of depraved racist inhumanity, he experienced compassion and solidarity and profound tearful sadness.... Could a contagion of tears rather than a contagion of rage be healing, could it restore hope in humanity? The answer seems clearly yes."[8]

But we must be careful to give rage the credit it deserves. It has a special power that is mighty enough to combat some of the strongest forces and systems at work in the world. In this book I argue that a particular type of anger, what I call Lordean rage, has an important role to play in anti-racist struggle. Taking its name from Audre Lorde, the Black feminist poet and scholar who first articulated the version of rage I'll be exploring, Lordean rage is targeted at racism. It tends toward metabolization and aims for change. It is informed by an inclusive and liberating perspective. An organizer who is angry at racial inequality and motivated to end it so that all of us, regardless of skin color, can flourish has Lordean rage. It is not an ideal type of anger. Rather, it is often experienced by the racially oppressed and their allies. Although Lordean rage may not be necessary, it can be uniquely used for anti-racist purposes.

When compared to the more generic notion of rage, it is less vulnerable to criticisms that it interferes with liberal goals and therefore should be replaced with more positive emotions. Instead, as I explain, Lordean rage does not preclude other emotional and cognitive responses like compassion and empathy. So, when a protestor marches in the street, their anger is expressing compassion for the downtrodden and love for justice. For this reason, I claim throughout this book that Lordean rage should not be discarded, suppressed, or replaced but rather managed—although my view on what this management entails parts with traditional notions.

My argument falls within the tradition of feminist philosophers who have argued for the intrinsic and instrumental value of anger in response to oppression. These philosophers have noted the appropriateness of anger in response to sexist oppression. They claim that it is a form of protest that may help women retain their self-respect, gain insight into their oppression, and bear witness to that oppression. It is also a way to claim one's love for good, and one's hatred for evil. Recent books written by activists and journalists on the rage of women in the context of the #MeToo movement also defend anger in the fight against sexism and misogyny. They point to how anger has been a motivating force in inspiring myriad responses to sexist oppression. I have learned a lot from these insights.

I am specifically concerned in this book, however, with anger in the context of racial oppression. Although a person could read the feminist literature and then decide to apply those insights into their own racial projects, I think that speaking explicitly to the specificity of people's lives and struggles is important. Just as oppressions have similarities, there are also dissimilarities. It's important that we recognize that our oppressions, social positions, and fights are multifarious. Thinking about what anger *distinctly* does in the context of racial injustice is a way of being attuned to these differences, and at the same time seeing them as illuminating rather than divisive. I am interested in what role anger distinctively plays in anti-racist struggle.

Anger plays the role of expressing the value of people of color and racial justice; it provides the eagerness, optimism, and self-belief needed to fight against persistent and powerful racist people and systems; and it allows the outraged to break certain racial rules as a form of intrinsic and extrinsic resistance. This helps explain how the oppressed can feel affirmed when others get angry on their behalf, how people are able to fight against powerful systems despite the risk of abuse and arrests, and why WNBA and NBA players—who used their platform to combat racism—were viewed as radical for simply expressing their feelings.

It is easy to assume that this is a book about "Black rage" but that is not the case. I recognize that Blacks are not the only victims of

racial oppression, nor are they the only people outraged about racial injustice. I am concerned with the anger of all people of color
and their allies—an anger directed at racism. I engage the African
American intellectual tradition more than any other, however;
African Americans (with the exception of Native peoples) have
had one of the longest relationships with US racism, and thus Black
thinkers provide us with a rich archive of reflections, analyses, and
exemplar actions that can help us think about anger and race. The
Black intellectual tradition that I rely on may at times seem both
typical and atypical. It may be surprising to some readers that my
account of anger is not based on radical male figures like Malcolm
X or Nat Turner, but Black feminist Audre Lorde. My examples of
freedom fighters who embraced anger are not limited to figures like
David Walker but also include Martin Luther King Jr. as well as Ida
B. Wells and Sojourner Truth. There are some people you may expect to hear from, but do not. The thinkers whom I engage in no way
exhaust the list of exemplars and scholars of anger at racial injustice.
Nevertheless, they are "a critical initial starting place"[9] in thinking
about anger and anti-racist struggle.

I write this book as a moral psychologist and philosopher of race.
This means that I am concerned with the nature of anger, its func-
tionality, and its cultivation in the context of racial oppression. While
I engage the work of historical figures and use social movements as
examples, this book is in no way an intellectual historical project. For
example, while Audre Lorde inspires my own account of appropriate
rage, I do not attempt to reconstruct her views or arguments on anger
by determining her commitments and reasons or the motivations
and influences driving them. Also, it is not my aim to describe how
anger has operated historically within certain social movements.
I do hope that this sampling of thinkers and movements might provide a deeper understanding about the role of anger in anti-racist
struggle and perhaps inspire deeper interests in their work.

I should also note that this book is meant to be a short, cross-
over book that appeals to the academic and activist, the philosopher and citizen. As a result, my aim is to be philosophically
grounded *and* accessible. Reflecting on the role of anger in the

anti-racist struggle is not simply an armchair exercise or an interesting philosophical problem. I am concerned with what my argument means beyond the ivory tower, so I have readers outside of academia—for example, the thousands who flooded the streets to protest police violence in spring 2020, recent in my memory as I write this—in mind. I also do not think that philosophers are the only folks who have insightful things to say about anger and race, and they should not be the only people who get to hear my own insights on anger and race either. In my work as a whole, I not only write to the public but engage their contributions and think with them. I do not apologize for these choices and believe they need no further explanation.

Two particularly important attitudes undergird this project that are worth mentioning here. The first is embracing the inevitability of racism and the need to be excellent practitioners of anti-racist struggle given this knowledge. This requires diligence in the face of perpetual struggle, knowing what's in one's control, and rejecting utopian prescriptions.[10] In that spirit, I am interested in looking at the role a nonideal emotion like anger plays in responding to a nonideal society. My approach rejects the idea that only positive emotions are the most effective and appropriate ones. One's resistant practices can still be justified and effective even when they are uncivil. As such, I accept that we need to expand our modes of principled resistance.[11] In that spirit, I accept that Lordean rage may not be pure, innocent, or civil, but this does not diminish its usefulness and appropriateness in anti-racist struggle, nor does it preclude other moral possibilities.

Overall, the aim of this book is to use the resources of moral psychology, ethics, philosophy of race, and social and political philosophy to make a case for Lordean rage's important role in anti-racist struggle. If I do this properly, it will influence some to, at least, not be so quick to recommend that we eliminate rage when racial wrongdoing grabs our public attention. The book shows that rage is not the problem—it is a *response* to the real problem. More importantly, the book shows the range of possible ways that many people have to respond powerfully and positively to racism with rage.

Remember, emotions are not what make us human, but theorizing about emotions is a distinct human activity. So let's get to theorizing about one of the most controversial emotions around—anger—and its place in the most controversial of contexts—racial injustice.

1
Painting in Broad Strokes

He is meant to be an example, his life a cautionary tale of what happens when you let anger control you—at least that's how many interpret the story. Whether you've read all 15,693 verses of Homer's epic poem *The Iliad* or used the cheat code by staring into Brad Pitt's dreamy eyes for three hours in the 2004 movie *Troy*, you may be somewhat familiar with the story of the Greek hero Achilles *and* his anger.

After feeling slighted when his bride was taken from him by his commander, Achilles—full of anger—temporarily leaves his own army. He refuses to continue to fight in the Trojan War and is tempted to return home. Since he is the real MVP of #TeamGreeks, many of his compatriots would die as he counted his grudges from the sidelines. In Achilles's absence, they would lose one battle after the other. *Rage can bring harm to those you care about.*

When Hector of #TeamTroy kills Achilles's best friend, only then does he return to battle. He avenges his friend's death. But he goes even further. Unable to tame his anger, Achilles desecrates his enemy's corpse, violating law and custom in battle. *Rage can make you lose your mind and morals.*

Or at least that's what we are made to think. This is the stereotypical image of anger. It's what most people think of when they think of it. Rage is untamed, lacks reason, and results in chaos. But those who hold this image of anger are making a mistake by thinking this is all that anger is. Anger can be a force for good on the battlefield for justice. We must remember this in the face of urges to abolish it altogether.

Give Anger a Chance

Often when we talk about anger, we paint it in broad strokes. That is to say, we generalize about anger as though it is one thing. The one image or portrait that we paint of anger looks something like the fictional villain Dr. Evil from Mike Myers's *Austin Powers* films. Dr. Evil—as the name implies—is a master of evil and he won't stop until he terrorizes and takes over the world. Similarly, anger in all forms is often illustrated in the same way. It is painted as a villain who has destructive powers and wields terror through whoever happens to be possessed by it, even great heroes like Achilles. It has no nuance, no upside. This generalized, one-dimensional, broad-strokes depiction of anger was first painted by ancient thinkers and is perpetuated by contemporary psychologists and philosophers. It has a long history. And it continues to be just as prevalent today as it was in years past.

The Stoic philosopher Seneca believed that anger "is above all other [emotions] hideous and wild, raging with an utterly inhuman lust for arms, blood and tortures. . . . Anger [is] a short madness: for it is equally devoid of self-control . . . forgetful of kinship."[1] Writing millennia later, psychologists would assert that the action tendency of anger (by which I mean behavior that a person is likely to engage in, given the anger) is retaliation and it "comes with an inclination to attack, humiliate, or otherwise get the person back who is perceived as acting unfairly or immorally."[2] On the philosophy side, some thinkers argue that the desire for retribution helps us to see "the irrationality and stupidity of anger."[3] Some of those who subscribe to the broad-strokes picture of anger as destructive and uncontrollable, even going back as far as eighth-century Buddhist sage Santideva, recommend its elimination. They think that we should replace anger with meekness or sadness. If we are angry, we should not be for long since revolutionary justice is best served by our transition from anger to generosity and love.[4]

Anger is often, although not always, painted in broad strokes, while other emotions are not. When we think of love, for example, we view it in its varieties. There is *philia*, which is brotherly love. There is also *agape*, which is universal love. Then there is romantic love, a love that involves the erotic. Love admits of varieties. There is also conditional and unconditional love, requited and unrequited love, as well as love for virtue and love for vice. Here too, love admits of varieties. These types have distinct targets and action tendencies. And the recognition of their distinctiveness allows us to not only see love's varieties and appreciate its different forms, but it provides us with adequate information to approve or disapprove of a particular type.

Similarly, we should look at anger in its varieties by taking on what I call the *image variation view*. This view appreciates the varieties and complexity that anger contains. In seeing anger in its varieties, we can appreciate that anger, particularly anger at racial injustice, is not necessarily destructive. If it is, it is only destructive to oppressive systems and not to life as we know it.

There is not just one type of anger but many. In the realm of political injustice, we can find at least five types of political anger. As we'll see, recognizing the nuances and types of political anger in all their richness, and thinking about how we can work with them rather than simply reject them, will lead to powerful and important change in our moral and political lives.

Other Variation Artists

Before I provide my own view of anger at racial injustice, it is important to point out that not every person who has written about anger has painted it broadly. A few philosophers have attempted to describe anger's varieties—although this is not a common philosophical move. I call them *variation artists*. We can categorize these thinkers' attempts by the kinds of distinctions they make—which they then use to help determine if the anger is good or bad.[5]

Those in the *concern distinction* camp classify types of anger by what the anger is about or what concerns it manifests. If the anger is about moral concerns, then generally speaking the anger is good.

If the anger is about immoral concerns, then the anger is bad. For example, virtuous anger is anger that manifests a concern for fairness, rights, equality, and the well-being of others.[6] Vicious anger manifests a lack of concern, ill will, or malice; this is the type of anger you probably think of first, given all its negative connotations. The former is usually captured in the language of "righteous indignation."

According to people in the *intent distinction* camp, we can classify anger as good or bad based on its wish or desire.[7] And that wish helps us determine if the anger is good or bad. Those in this camp think that anger types like payback, pain-passing, and recognition-respect anger differ in what we intend when we are angry.[8] I intend to cause harm when I have payback anger. I intend to cause pain on those who are not responsible for my pain when I have pain-passing anger. And I intend to restore my sense of dignity by making demands for respect when I have recognition-respect anger. Out of these three, it is the latter type that we are more likely to approve of morally. We are less inclined to think that payback or projection is acceptable.

People in the *type distinction* camp believe that anger is very black-and-white. They view types of anger as dichotomies, with one bad and the other good. For example, there is sudden anger and deliberative anger.[9] The former is irrational, partial, and aims at destruction. The latter is rational, impartial, and aims at justice. There's also a contrast between garden-variety anger and transition anger.[10] While garden-variety anger involves protest and payback, transition anger has the protest minus the payback aspect. It takes a stand against wrongdoing but doesn't aim for revenge. Instead, as the anger transitions to love, it aims for generosity. The Greek philosopher Aristotle is also a part of this camp, perhaps its founder. He makes a distinction between anger that lies according to what he calls the mean and anger that does not. Moderated anger is directed at the right thing, at the right time, and to the right degree. Unmoderated anger—you might guess—is all over the place.

I am a variation artist like the aforementioned philosophers. But although their distinctions improve on the broad-strokes view, they do not in fact articulate the various elements of political anger—particularly anger at racial injustice—that concern me. Nor do they explain how the distinctions they describe naturally go together. None of these possible ways of distinguishing between different types of anger gives us relevant dimensions to describe *and* evaluate anger at racial injustice in particular. This is what is missing.

My aim, though, is not to give my own theoretical account of anger. I am only focused on introducing new categories from which to distinguish political anger types and thus evaluate them properly. Once we know what kind of anger helps drive racial justice, we can pursue and cultivate it without any worry that it's the kind of anger that we want to avoid.

Some Preliminary Points

So how should we distinguish among types of anger in a way that points us toward the types that will lead to racial justice and away from those that will not? We can focus on the *target, action tendency,* and *aim* of the anger, as well as the *perspective* that informs the anger. These dimensions are sufficient in distinguishing varieties of anger and determining if a particular variety is good or bad, in the sense of productive or unproductive when it comes to the pursuit of justice— especially racial justice. By "target" I am referring to whom the anger is directed at: yourself, your friend, maybe your country or a certain policy.[11] By "aim" I mean what a person hopes to achieve in a way that is somehow connected to being angry (e.g., the purposes and plans that the anger naturally tends to lead to). The perspective that informs the anger refers to an attitude or way of thinking from which the anger arises.

You may be wondering: is it the person who feels the rage who has a particular aim, or is the aim a function of the emotion? Well, it's both. Emotions motivate us to act in a certain way. They can also influence our beliefs and desires. Yes, we can act or not act, and the emotion can only do its thing through us and in partnership with us. If I say the action tendency of anger is to approach a target, I simply mean that the anger motivates us to do so. What we eventually do is up to us. When I talk about aims, I am talking about emotions influencing our desires and goals. How we allow this desire to influence our behavior is up to us.

My intention is not to describe and defend or criticize every type of anger. To accomplish this task requires more space than this book can provide. This is not to say that my categories are not useful for creating a more generalized account of anger's varieties. It is only to admit my limited focus. My main task is to offer some varieties of anger (defined by the four categories I described earlier) in the context of racial injustice. As I've said, the varieties that I introduce are within the sphere of political anger in general and racial injustice in particular. (I am writing this in the summer of 2020, when the connection between anger and racial justice is maybe more at the top of more readers' minds than it would have been in 2019 or any year before, as protests and other activism reached a crescendo across the United States when many could no longer hold inside their anger at police violence, among other race-based injustices in our country.)

Moreover, the variations that I describe are not exhaustive. We can add other types to the list, but for brevity I only focus on five. We can also add more positive variations, but here I only present one. These distinctions are also not neat. Some variations can have features of another. They can overlap, even run into or transition to the others. The perspective of the rage is also a huge source of the rage. How I think about myself and others will have an impact on the anger I have. A white supremacist and civil rights leader are unlikely to share the same anger, and this has a lot to do with their dissimilar social outlooks. While the anger is paradigmatically born of these perspectives, if you can change the worldview perhaps the anger will change. As we will see, changes in perspective—for example, coming to believe that Black lives do matter—can sometimes cause changes in the kind of anger that we feel.

These variations are also not group essential—by which I mean they are not restricted, by definition, to certain racial groups. I needn't be a member of a particular racial group in order to experience a specific type of anger. And just because I belong to a certain racial group doesn't mean that I will always experience one type of anger over another. An Arab person and an African American person could share the same type of anger. A white Brit and Black South African could also share the same type of anger. While I provide historical and present-day examples of each account, we should not think that only one racial group can experience one particular type of anger.

Finally, I describe these variations mostly by using the term *rage* instead of *indignation* or *anger*. While it can be said that the use of *rage* points to the irrational, uncontrolled, and dangerous nature of anger in politically charged contexts, at least in a colloquial sense, I do not use the term with reference to this kind of pejorative reputation. Instead, it is following in the tradition of race scholars who embrace the term "Black rage," including bell hooks and Cornel West, as well as feminist scholars like Soraya Chemaly and Brittney Cooper, who use "rage" to describe the anger of women under a patriarchal society. I use the term as a synonym for anger. This rage is not by definition an unbridled anger, rather it is an intense anger in response to incessant injustice. Since I provide anger types that fit this description, "rage" is the term I'll favor.

A Look at Five Varieties

Rogue Rage

Christian Picciolini was fourteen years old when he became a member of a violent neo-Nazi organization.[12] What drew him? By his own account, he was a young white man who felt marginalized, angry, and broken. Through his band, White American Youth, he would go on for eight years to create music that inspired listeners to engage in acts of violence. He also participated in this violence. It served as a vehicle where he and others could project their anger and pain onto innocent people who they thought were responsible for their problems. Christian was not only a white supremacist. He was also a rogue rager.

Rogue rage is anger at injustice, although the target of the anger is not necessarily the person or institution that caused the injustice. A person with rogue rage blames almost everyone for his unjust experiences. His anger is directed at them because almost everyone—at least according to the rogue rager—is responsible for the injustice he senses.

Given this "me versus everyone else" positioning, those with rogue rage have an action tendency to isolate themselves. This doesn't mean that they decide to be alone and angry. They may decide instead to isolate themselves from the general society but opt into small communities that share in their rage, either online or in person. In this way they "go rogue."

The aim of rogue rage is not to find a resolution to experiences of injustice. Those with rogue rage are not looking for new laws to be enacted, polices to be reformed, funding to be distributed, or authorities to listen to their demands for change. This is because the resolution isn't what interests them. Their only aim is to hit back at the world for supposedly hitting at them first. Often this response is physical violence; other times it is not. And the victims of their response are likely to be anyone and everyone. It's not surprising that people like young Christian Picciolini would engage in random acts of violence. Only by hitting back in this kind of way can rogue ragers find any relief or satisfaction.

Rogue ragers do not aim for or think that there can be a resolution, and this is partly because the perspective that informs rogue rage is nihilism. Nihilism is a sense of dread and despair, an absence of belief or hope, that, according to activist and scholar Cornel West, "results from forms of soul craft that put a premium on conquest and domination, mendacity and criminality."[13] In nihilism, hope, meaning, and self-worth dwindle.[14]

Recognizing that rogue rage comes from this nihilistic perspective helps us make sense of rogue rage's lack of aim for change. If a person does not have any hope that things will get better, he is less likely to aim and thus work to get it. Examples of rogue rage can include the rage of racist terrorists, but it can equally be racist internet trolls—they act to provoke a response rather than to seek particular resolution to what fuels their rage in the first place.

Wipe Rage

Around one thousand people, consisting of white nationalists, neo-Nazis, and other members of the alt-right and other far-right groups, descended on the campus of the University of Virginia in the summer of 2017 to protest the removal of a Confederate statue of Robert E. Lee. Decked in polo shirts and carrying tiki torches, white men and women marched chanting anti-Black and anti-Semitic statements like, "You will not replace us!" The phrase refers to the belief that whites are on the verge of extinction by nonwhites—and something must be done about it. Their march not only expressed fear, hatred, and desires for white power. It also expressed wipe rage.

Some people may feel a sense of injustice because of their race. They may experience economic disparities and feel ignored by a government system that is supposed to represent and serve them. In response to the injustice, they may experience rage that is aimed at wiping out or eliminating the other. Though this may sound just like rogue rage, it is quite different from it.

The targets of wipe rage are not anyone and everyone, nor are they economic leaders or the government. Racial "others" are the targets. This is not simply a case of pain-passing—where the outraged passes on the pain that they have experienced to those who are not the cause of it. On the contrary, those with wipe rage believe that the racial other *is* the cause of their experiences of injustice and they are often resistant to information that proves the contrary. In this way, the targets of wipe rage are scapegoats. (Think of people who are unemployed, or see the problems in the US job market and blame immigrants from Mexico for "taking our jobs.")

The action tendency of those with wipe rage is to eliminate the scapegoats. This action tendency is possible because of the hatred directed at scapegoats. When we hate others, we often want them to be eliminated.[15] This elimination need not be physical. Those with wipe rage can desire the scapegoats' social death; to take the example of immigrants and jobs, they would aim at the expulsion of immigrants from their country and the banning of future immigration. In other, darker examples, the words "elimination" and "death" are not metaphorical but literal, as with Jews and other marginalized groups whom the Nazis aimed to eliminate entirely in the Holocaust. Elimination is both an action tendency of wipe rage and an aim and goal for its targets.

The perspective that informs wipe rage is a zero-sum-game way of thinking. In this perspective, there is only one winner and one loser. If you win, then I lose. If I win, then you lose. To ensure that my racial group wins (e.g., gains economic advances), another racial group must lose (e.g., face economic setbacks). Those with wipe rage fail to see that justice is a win-win game. When one group makes advancements, other groups are able to as well.

Ressentiment Rage

Ressentiment rage may sound strange at first, perhaps even redundant. "Ressentiment" is the French translation of the English word "resentment," even though it does not perfectly latch on to what we take resentment to be in English.[16] But what do I mean by the term?

Ressentiment rage is aimed at a racial group in power and is expressed by those who are without power. It is likely to be directed at all members of the powerful group. I am thinking of an Indigenous person who is angry at *all* white people in America. Given that the racial group in power obtained power through some form of struggle with the now-outraged (genocide in the case of Native peoples), the aim for those with ressentiment rage is revenge. The outraged wishes for revenge as payback for the racial group taking away his group's power. And he may wish for and even cause physical, mental, or status harm as a result. But the outraged also envies his target—for a part of him wishes he was in power. Imagine the Indigenous person who hates all white people, but also wishes he had white people's exploitative power.

The action tendency of ressentiment rage is reactivity. People with ressentiment rage are reactive in the world, always playing defense or making up lost ground—pick a metaphor. In being reactive, they are subjects acted upon. They define themselves only against the other. For example, a person who is reactive only sees himself as confident when he makes others feel insecure or he sees himself as wonderful only when he views others as inferior. Reactive people can only see themselves as a response to and in opposition to others. The Indigenous person, for example, can feel self-respect only by disrespecting whites.

Those with ressentiment rage do not act in the world. People act on them. In being active, on the other hand, a person doesn't require others to be small for him to be big. In addition, he takes something as his object and uses creativity to create the world. He creates a world full of values and improvements.

The perspective that informs ressentiment rage is that the oppressive group is the standard. This "reactive" preoccupation with the powerful racial group makes the oppressor the point of reference. It defines the terms in which the outraged think and act (making any response that they have more akin to reactivity rather than activity). This makes the outraged think of and judge themselves against the racial, dominating other. The powerful becomes the outraged's obsession. And the outraged's eye becomes focused on the powerful group and not on their own flourishing future.[17] Another example of ressentiment rage could be the colonized who might both want to enact revenge on the colonizers while envying them at the same time.

Narcissistic Rage

In August 2018 a white man, Dr. Jeffrey Epstein, was detained by police at an Orlando airport for being unruly. As police forced him to the ground, Epstein screamed, "You're being rough with me! You're treating me like a f*cking Black person." Recognizing the irony but also the asymmetry between his perceived treatment and the treatment of Black folks, the subtitle of the *GQ* article covering this incident read, "Despite This, He Was Not Shot."[18] While there are several ways that we could read the viral video, the second part of his reaction is worth analysis. Though the statement could be quickly read as an analogy of mistreatment, it points to—at least as I see things—narcissistic rage.

bell hooks coined the term *narcissistic rage* in her 1995 book *Killing Rage*. An example of people she describes as having this rage are Black elites. She notes that when some Black elites arc outraged, it is not at white supremacy that exploits and oppresses Black people. Rather, they are outraged because although they have worked hard and risen through the ranks—gaining much social capital and even acceptance by some whites—they face the reality that "they are not exempt from racist assault."[19] A sense of exceptionalism and not a sense of systemic injustice motivates the rage. These Black elites are outraged because their perceived exemption status has not been taken seriously. And it has not been given uptake because oppressive powers refuse to make a distinction between them and other members of the oppressed group.

In this way, hooks's analysis and example map onto the Orlando airport situation. Narcissistic rage can apply to people at opposite ends of the privileged scale. So let's flesh out narcissistic rage a little more.

Who is the target of narcissistic rage? It is not oppressive forces, institutional racism, or white supremacy. The target is "those who target me." In other words, those who are narcissistically outraged are not angry at racial injustice and forces that enact, enforce, and are complicit in it. Instead, they are mad at only those forces that target them as individuals. They are mad at the police who target them and not a biased police department that may also target a particular community. They are not angry at a white supremacist system that discriminates against certain immigrants. Rather, they are angry at a system that doesn't allow people *like them* individually to succeed—or yell freely at an airport.

The action tendency of those who are narcissistically outraged is to express their place within a particular hierarchy. Part of their protest involves proclaiming and reiterating their place within the overall system. So, unsurprisingly, they express that they "are not a Black person" or at least not like the nonelite ones. (Not surprisingly, this does little to advance the anti-racist cause.) This tendency also reveals an indifference to the sufferings of others—because the kinds of injustice or mistreatment that they are experiencing are only relevant given that they are the victims. They are indifferent to those who are suffering under the same oppressive system.

We see this phenomenon not only across racial and class lines, but based on gender and sexual orientation as well. Those with narcissistic rage may think that the only Black lives that matter are straight Black men—or maybe even specifically their own Black life. They are indifferent to violence against Black trans and cis women. And the expression of their narcissistic rage is to signal the hierarchal place of straight Black men above Black trans and cis women. This is comparable to the narcissistic rage that leads cis white feminists to agitate for equality for "women," when they are only trying to advance the rights of women just like themselves—not women of color or trans women.

There are other options on the table. In hooks's view, the narcissistically outraged could link their rage to "progressive challenge and critique of white supremacy rooted in solidarity with the [other] masses."[20] But instead they focus on themselves, their privilege, and their status. This reveals that the aim of narcissistic rage is not to change a racist system, dismantle privilege, or fight for the unheard. Rather, the aim is "justice . . . just for me." The aim of narcissistic rage is for the outraged to be treated better than those who fall outside of their level of privilege.

The perspective that underlies narcissistic rage is not merely excessive self-importance, although those who have this rage will feel that they are more important than others. But it is also an egocentric self-entitlement that determines what, for whom, and to what extent they are outraged. The perspective that a person is a special case, separate and different from all others, and should be treated accordingly is what informs narcissistic rage.

* * *

Given the targets, aims, action tendencies, and perspectives of rogue, wipe, ressentiment, and narcissistic rage, we can clearly see why these types of rage are morally and politically problematic and why they should be criticized. And by being problematic in the particular ways we've seen, they bring shame to rage's name—especially for those who are so hasty that they paint it in broad strokes. The diverse categorical distinctions I have provided help us see why this is the case. Remember, wipe rage aims to eliminate others through hate, ressentiment rage reproduces oppressive actions, and narcissistic rage shows an indifference to the suffering of others and projects a sense of superiority. These aims and tendencies are not only unethical but can produce harmful effects in the world. But not all anger looks like them. While we can see how these variations might obstruct racial justice and even perpetuate injustice, another variation stands out from all the rest that deserves our attention. It is our best hope.

Lordean Rage

Lordean rage contrasts with the other types of rage in stark ways. It is this anger type that I explore and make the case for throughout the rest of this book. Named after the Black feminist scholar and poet Audre Lorde (and based on my reading of her essays on anger and race), Lordean rage, as I conceive of it, is a type that plays an important role in anti-racist struggle and is not necessarily destructive. (From here on, know that when I refer to "rage" or "anti-racist anger," I'm speaking about Lordean rage in particular.) Although I use Lorde's work about anger and race to help theorize Lordean rage, the conception of Lordean rage is my own.

Lorde defines *racism* as "the belief in the inherent superiority of one race over all others and thereby the right to dominance, manifest and implied."[21] The targets of Lordean rage are those who are complicit in and perpetrators of racism and racial injustice. This type of anger is directed at racist actions, racist attitudes, and presumptions (of people) that arise out of those attitudes. These needn't come from powerful forces from afar. These attitudes and actions can (and often do) come from people who profess solidarity with the racially marginalized.

The action tendency of Lordean rage is to absorb and use it for energy. As the title of Lorde's influential essay "Uses of Anger" suggests, anger has its benefits. And Lordean rage is useful if it is focused with precision and translated into needed action. In this way, Lordean rage is metabolized anger—"the virtuous channeling of the power and energy of anger without the desire to harm or pass pain."[22] It is a call to "fight injustice and respect the reality of one's anger without being destroyed by it."[23]

Note that this anger is *transformative anger* and not *transition anger*.[24] For Martha Nussbaum in particular—in her 2016 book *Anger and Forgiveness*—revolutionary justice can only occur after anger transitions to generosity and love. Lordean rage, on the other hand, doesn't need to disappear or transition to something else in order to achieve certain results. Instead, it is morally, politically, and epistemically useful for transformative ends as it is. Put another way, rogue, wipe, and narcissistic rage do look like the kinds of anger that need to be replaced with something else before you can have sustained progress (even if they might be useful for justice in a sporadic, contingent, lucky way now and then). But Lordean rage is a kind that is well suited to maintain itself just as it is, without needing to get out of the way so that "better" emotions can get to work.

At what is Lordean rage aimed? Its aim is change. Change could mean to make worse or to return to a previous, unjust state. Those who marched in Charlottesville, Virginia, for example, wanted America to return to its racist past. But Lorde helps us to see that the change she was concerned with was not "a simple switch of positions or a temporary lessening of tensions, nor the ability to smile or feel good." It is instead "a basic and radical alteration in all those assumptions underlining our lives."[25] Lordean rage aims for this kind of change—not destruction of the good or elimination of the other, but change in racist beliefs, expectations, policies, and behaviors that shape and support white supremacy. This anti-racist rage can be used to engage in action that brings about such a change.

The perspective that informs Lordean rage is best put in Lorde's own words: "I am not free while any [other] is unfree." Freedom is not exclusive. It is inclusive. And those who desire it in this way embrace those whose "shackles are different from our own" rather than selected members of a particular group.[26] Lorde was not only concerned about justice for well-educated Black women like herself. She was also concerned about the poor and those in developing nations. We can learn from this.

This inclusive perspective helps us to see that if we fail to "recognize them as other faces of [ourselves]," then we are contributing not only to their oppressions but also to our own.[27] This makes Lordean rage quite different from narcissistic and wipe rage. Absent this perspective, the outraged are only fighting for "their own" and the rage is bound to be destructive since it is indifferent to the sufferings of others. Without this perspective, the outraged may see others as the cause of their own suffering when instead they are fellow sufferers, themselves outraged for other reasons. But Lordean rage's inclusivity allows it to escape some of the poisons of the other variations and reach its goal.

Someone might think that in developing my account of Lordean rage, I have just picked all the potentially positive features of anger and packaged them. Why are the features I have attached to Lordean rage what they are—naturally? Well, I think these features are naturally bundled together for several reasons. When your anger is a response to racism (a widespread phenomenon, system, and structure), you or one other person are never the only victims. Your response to racism is a response to all of those fallen victims. Therefore, the perspective that informs it is likely to be freedom for all, even if you and those close to you are no longer vulnerable to racism. And since anger, in general, has an approach action tendency (more on this in Chapter 3), the person with Lordean rage would aim to tackle racism head-on by seeking to change the world, so that racism is no more.

This helps us see why the features of the other types of rage, like narcissistic rage, are also naturally bundled. If a person is only angry at racial injustice when it affects them and no one else, this says a lot about what they think about themselves and what they aim to do. If I am indifferent to the sufferings of other people who look like me, but not my own suffering, perhaps I think that something is special or unique about me. In a racial schema, perhaps I think I am the exception, superior. This will affect what I believe, desire, and aim to do. So, it makes sense that narcissistic rage would have the features it has.

This is not to say that Lordean rage is by definition virtuous and that, if it goes wrong, we cannot criticize it since at such a failure point, it ceases to be Lordean rage. Lordean rage manifests with a particular set of features and is likely to go right, but it can go wrong in a limited number of cases for understandable or foreseeable reasons. (I say more about this in Chapter 2.) For example, Lordean rage can go wrong when I invest my full emotional life in responding to wrongdoers at the neglect of loving and being attentive to those with whom I am in solidarity. In this case, it causes me to abandon people who are in my circle of concern. Lordean rage can also go wrong when it causes me to abandon not only other-directed care but also self-care. The outraged person can be so angry at injustice and motivated to pursue justice for all that she neglects tending to her own psychological needs. Also, since racial injustice is persistent, the temptation to constantly express and act in response to this rage—at all times, no matter how productive—can burden the outraged person.[28] If Lordean rage leads a person to think they must fight every fight, never taking a break to recover, it can cause burnout and distress. So Lordean rage being apt or fitting depends on circumstances.

You may have noticed that I have not talked about feel, intensity, or duration within these accounts. This may lead you to assume that I do not think these political anger types have any unique feel to them, for example. And if they have no feel, then why should we call them anger? The omission was intentional. But the reasoning is quite different from what you might assume.

I have omitted giving attention to the categories of feel, intensity, and duration because, while I admit they are present in these varieties of anger, I do not think they determine, in definitive ways, what makes one variation different from the others. A person with wipe rage may experience the same phenomenological feel of anger as the person with rogue rage. A person's narcissistic rage may be as intense as someone else's Lordean rage. A person's ressentiment rage may last as long as someone's wipe rage. Even if the intensity of rogue rage is stronger than wipe rage, I do not think this says anything significant about endorsing it or not, nor whether it has good political uses. More must be said, and I hope that my explanation of these various types of rage has at least begun to address this.

The image variation view gives us additional information to determine whether the anger critics are right or wrong about their generalized picture of anger as necessarily bad. It gives us a clearer picture of what anger can look like within a political context of racial concerns. But it also helps us see where the mistakes of the anger critics lie. The real target of anger critics is not anger. It is actually only *some* anger variations. Lordean rage is one variation (among possible others) that escapes their criticisms.

Who Can Experience Lordean Rage?

You might be wondering at this point if Lordean rage is just virtuous Aristotelian anger with a political, anti-racist twist. And if it is what some people might then call *noble rage*, is it also—in Aristotle's sense—something that only the virtuous person can have and sustain? I understand the worry behind this question. It may seem that Lordean rage is not something to which we're naturally given. It also seems that it will be hard work for many to become the kind of person who can have Lordean rage. Is Lordean rage, then, an exclusive emotion that only a few noble souls are capable of feeling?

Thankfully, the answer is no. It's easy to think that Lordean rage is not something to which we are *naturally* given. What we are naturally given to when we are angry at a sibling, for example, is a desire to hit or lash out at them. In this way, you might accept that the *natural* action tendency of anger is retaliation, and any opposing tendency is either superhuman or supervirtuous. However, this kind of thinking stems from a broad-strokes picture of anger, which, as we've seen, leads us astray. More specifically, it says that anger motivates us in only one way. I am trying to challenge this very idea. As I show in the next few chapters, many people, motivated by Lordean rage, have engaged in positive action, thereby showing that we are all capable of Lordean rage.

Does Lordean rage require me to be a noble soul? I do not think so. I could have a destructive kind of anger directed at my brother and a constructive kind of anger directed at racists. (Both kinds of anger can coexist in me—I contain multitudes!) The presence of the former may show that I'm not so morally perfect after all. It doesn't cancel out the possibility of Lordean rage directed at racists. To put it simply, Lordean rage does not require the extremely hard moral work that we think it does or more character work than other emotions like compassion. Yes, it stands in sharp contrast to a rage that aims to eliminate others based on hate (wipe rage). But this doesn't mean that to then direct our anger at racists requires something as extreme as moral perfection. It may require that we recognize wrongdoing. But it doesn't require that we have excellence of character in order to aim for change. Maybe all we need to have is the desire for something morally and politically better. In other words, it's possible that Lordean rage may require us to have moral sensitivity and moral imagination, but not necessarily moral excellence. It is within reach.

Now, for some people, their natural dispositions and social positioning may make them more suited for Lordean rage. For example, those whose lives are more socially vulnerable may be more likely to respond with Lordean rage given their intersectional understanding and thus their acceptance of the perspective that informs Lordean rage (I am not free until we all are free). It is therefore not surprising that the figure who inspired my account of anger—Audre Lorde—is a Black lesbian. Lorde had an intersectional understanding of oppression and was aware of the ways that oppression can negatively affect everyone. Also, a person who is optimistic or proactive may be more likely to respond with Lordean rage given their view of the world and their disposition to actively engage with it. But dispositions are not synonymous with moral traits of perfection.

Lastly, there are three practical reasons why we should resist the idea that only noble souls can exhibit Lordean rage. For Aristotle, the virtuous man is rare. Virtue or excellence of character is something we aim for, but rarely achieve. Lordean rage is not rare, however. It is attainable and there are many examples of it out in the world. (I have not written this book for the rare breed or the emotional equivalent of W. E. B. Du Bois's famous "Talented Tenth," but for lots of ordinary folks who have, in many instances already, experienced Lordean rage.)

If Lordean rage requires a noble soul and being noble is rare, it may be hard for people to recognize Lordean rage when it appears or may easily dismiss it when it appears—referring to it as narcissistic or rogue rage—based on its perceived rarity. They may think that Lordean rage's rarity gives us decisive reasons to default to doubt when it appears. This presents an additional roadblock to achieving the emotional intelligence of which I am trying to persuade readers. (More on this later.)

We also need to be careful not to paint those with Lordean rage as moral saints—people we should admire but can never hope to be. Doing so can make us think that we are off the moral hook from acting in certain ways and are therefore justified in retreating into indifference, or wipe or ressentiment rage. But if we think about Lordean rage as something exceptional and rare, we can make the mistake of thinking that those who are *more likely* to have Lordean rage (the oppressed) are moral saints. While this may sound positive, it can become another way of making them the other, and setting them apart. While giving people moral credit is not disrespectful, it can feed into the trope of the oppressed as morally virtuous people whose virtue alone will save us *all*. This is a lot to put on the shoulders of those already oppressed. People with Lordean rage "are not goddesses or matriarchs . . . fiery fingers of judgment," but have simply "learned to use anger."[29] We can all learn to use anger. Lordean rage is attainable for everyone. Painting people with Lordean rage as moral saints also sets a really high bar for how the oppressed must act—a bar we do not set for those in power. Another injustice is perpetuated when you have to be morally perfect to be an acceptable person of color but can just be your average (moral) Joe if you're white.

Why Does This Matter?

I have not provided these varieties in order to fight with critics of anger or to indulge in the game of making distinctions for distinctions' sake. (This is something for which analytic philosophers are known.) Rather, I think that taking an image variation view instead of a broad-strokes picture matters for our moral and political lives.

It allows us to have a more nuanced conversation about political anger. Instead of constantly debating whether a case of anger is good or bad, we can talk about several variations of anger and discuss not merely their goodness or badness but their targets, action tendencies, aims, and perspectives. Trust me, this makes for a more interesting discussion.

The image variation view can also help us improve our emotional intelligence. Emotional intelligence is the capacity to be aware of, express, and control our emotions. It is also the ability to effectively respond to others. The more we know what we could be feeling, the more we are able to name it. This will also help us in how we respond to others. Instead of simply judging any manifestation of anger as destructive, we can identify the variation or a particular category and respond to it more appropriately than if we only had the broad-strokes view.

This view also helps us embrace emotional diversity. Emotional diversity, as I see it, is recognizing that we are unique, and that not all people have the disposition to experience the same emotions in response to the same cause. While some people may respond to racial injustice with sadness or compassion, others may respond with anger. Emotional diversity makes room for expressions of a variety of fitting emotions in response to a particular cause—emotions that are not only targeted toward wrongdoers but also victims.

The point here is not that everyone *should* be angry. This would be an unfair argument to make, since we cannot will ourselves to feel any emotion. I cannot decide at this moment to be sad. This is not to say that I cannot participate in activities that might help me generate the emotion, like recalling a traumatic event or watching a dramatic television series or the news. Still there are no guarantees that these activities will generate the emotion. To therefore say *I should feel* any particular emotion at a particular time seems impossible even just based on a mild "ought implies can" principle (meaning that in order to be able to say you ought to do something you have to be able to do that thing in the first place). Likewise, I do not think that anyone should argue that we *should never* feel anger since, as I argue in Chapter 2, not only is it an emotion that arises as a response to wrongdoing but it can also be a fitting and morally appropriate response to racial wrongdoing. We should be able to feel a variety of apt emotions in response to wrongdoing.

Anger is a *fitting emotion* to wrongdoing, although it is not the *only fitting emotion*. We might include other emotions like countercontempt, an emotion that is a response to the vices of arrogance and pride.[30] We might also include emotions such as compassion, which is a response to victims. Emotional diversity allows for a variety of emotional experiences and expressions that can provide myriad forms of attentiveness, motivation, communication, and action. Anger makes us attentive to wrongdoing and motivates us to pursue justice. Compassion is a response to victims, and it motivates us to be attentive to them. Emotional diversity is important because it allows us to attend to several relevant parties and be motivated to respond in a variety of ways, among other things. What I hope the image variation view makes room for is the freedom to experience anger variations. Here I offer one positive option to aim for from a sea of morally problematic ones.

If we embrace emotional diversity, this makes room for tactical diversity in the fight against racial injustice. Tactical diversity is the ability to employ several actions to defeat an opponent. For example, to succeed as a mixed martial arts fighter, just knowing how to box will not do. It will be advantageous for the fighter to also know jujitsu or muay thai—other fighting styles. In this way, she can have a variety of tools in her arsenal to defeat her opponent. This can also be applied to fights against racism. Lordean rage won't be the best tool for everyone to use in combating all occasions of racial injustice, but it is among one of the best options, as we'll see.

All these together can help those committed to anti-racism achieve justice and equality. Compassion, as a response to wrongdoing, informs the ways in which we might respond to and deal with wrongdoing. For example, compassionate tactics may include more education for the offender and compensation efforts for the victim. And anger tactics may include blaming politicians and pressuring them to pass legislation. Combined, these tactics, although different in the results they achieve, provide a variety of ways to respond to injustice. The inclusion of a particular anger variety as a response to racial wrongdoing puts more tactical options on the table.

If all of this sounds tenable, then what should we do next? Recall that in the beginning of this chapter, I said that a broad-strokes picture of anger impacts the actions a person recommends. If anger is necessarily evil, then you might suggest that we eliminate or replace it. But based on the image variation view, we now have reasons why some variations are more morally concerning than others. If an anger is likely to go right, then eliminating and replacing all anger should not be our default options.

Lordean rage is not just acceptable—it is what we need desperately. We should cultivate it, guard it, and use it in anti-racist struggle. Why and how we should do this will become clear soon.

2
Fitting Fury, Rightful Rage

A Tale of Two Protests

In 2015, racial incidents at US college campuses were followed by a wave of student protests—most notably at Yale University and the University of Missouri at Columbia (Mizzou). Yale protests began after top administrators composed a series of emails. The university originally sent an email encouraging students to avoid racially insensitive Halloween costumes like blackface, turbans, and Native American dress. The email's aim was to call for students to be sensitive, thoughtful, and respectful of each other, particularly of those who are culturally different from them. (The school is 44 percent white, 13 percent Asian, 9 percent Latino, and 5 percent Black.[1]) But soon after, lecturer Erika Christakisr—in response to the email—argued that the university should give a little space for students to be provocative, inappropriate, and offensive. In disagreement with Christakisr's email, Black students—in an open letter—argued that they had a right to be respected. They believed that respect was not the same as coddling, nor was coddling what they were requesting. The open letter was followed by protests. The lecturer's email was not the first event that began to sow seeds of the students' rage, however. It was only the straw that broke the camel's back. Students had been angry long before that Halloween.

There were not only built-up racial problems at Yale but also a pattern of silence on behalf of the administration, according to some students. There were reports of "chronic racism" on campus, and it had caused students to feel psychologically and physically unsafe.[2] Prior to the email incident, there was a long list of documented racial problems. Most recently, Black women had been denied entry to a fraternity party on the grounds that it was a "white woman only" party. A Black student was held at gunpoint by campus police because the officer did not believe he was a student. Administrators, despite vocal concerns, refused—for decades—to rename a residence building that had been named after a white supremacist and defender of slavery. Swastikas were also found on campus. Still, in light of all of this, the administration remained silent. Black students and those in solidarity with them were angry. They had anti-racist anger targeted at these racial incidents, aimed at changing things at their university, and informed by the idea that all students deserved respect. They metabolized their anger to raise awareness and to pressure the administration to do better.

About the same time, similar protests were happening at Mizzou—a school only 110 miles from Ferguson, Missouri—the town where Michael Brown, an unarmed Black teenager, was shot and killed by police one year prior. At the same time as the Halloween protests at Yale, Black students at Mizzou reported several incidents in which racial slurs were hurled at them. Payton Head, a Black senior, reported comments that had been directed at him from a pickup truck. Documenting his experience online he wrote, "I really just want to know why my simple existence is such a threat to society. . . . For those of you who wonder why I'm always talking about the importance of inclusion and respect, it's because I've experienced moments like this multiple times at THIS university, making me not feel included here." While members of the Legion of Black Collegians were rehearsing on campus, a white Mizzou student called them a racial slur. Like Head, members responded online: "It's happened again. Just last night, on Traditions Plaza. Hate and racism were alive and well at Mizzou."[3] And when words proved insufficient, unknown perpetrators used symbols instead—drawing a swastika in feces in a campus bathroom.

It was not only the racial climate on campus. Mizzou students were also angry about what they took to be inadequate responses from the school administration. An infamous videotaped example of the latter shows student protestors blocking President Tim Wolfe's car as he refuses to get out and talk with them. A week later he would meet with students, but for some it was too little too late. A student would soon go on a hunger strike until the president resigned, and thirty-four Black members of the football team would join the protest. The resignation was important for students because, according to the Missouri Students Association, "[Wolfe] ha[d] not only enabled a culture of racism since the start of his tenure in 2012, but blatantly ignored and disrespected the concerns of students."[4] The president eventually resigned, and some of the students' demands were met. In the immediate aftermath, a bomb threat was sent with the words, "I will kill every Black person in sight." Two years later a report indicated that Black freshman enrollment had dropped by 42 percent.[5]

* * *

For the most part, critics of the angry student protestors did not *directly* attack what they took to be the students' rage. Instead, they resorted to a different strategy. First Amendment advocates reframed the protests as being about free speech, not racism.[6] Students had a legitimate complaint about the racist things people were doing on campus, but advocates reframed it to emphasize the rights of the people doing them. So rather than acknowledge racism, the focus was shifted to the ways in which the people committing the racist acts were doing something (legally) permissible. Also, angry students had a legitimate complaint about what people were doing on campus, but media coverage reframed it to emphasize the manner of the students' expression.[7]

The reframing in both instances took the focus away from the students' complaints and their legitimacy and toward permissible speech or politeness. If critics focused on the actual target of the angry protests (racism), they would run up against some difficulties with challenging the reality of racism and, thus, the appropriateness of the students' rage and its correct representation of what was happening.

The students were right to be angry; if their critics had engaged the substance, and not just the style, of their complaints, they would have seen this. When the cause and the target are racism, feeling rage makes sense. Such rage against racism—rage like these students felt, rage like protestors in a long list of uprisings against racism before and since these incidents have felt—is *fitting, appropriate,* and *correct*. We can hold anti-racist anger up to the most rigorous standard for assessing whether it is all these things and see how it meets and indeed surpasses the criteria.

Fit and Representation Matter

To say an emotion is fitting is to say that it makes sense to feel it toward a particular kind of thing. For example, if the emotion is in response to a genuine moral wrongdoing, then anger is a fitting response to that wrongdoing. Anger is an emotional response that *fits* the occurrence called wrongdoing.

When Bob gets angry that someone stole his television, we can say that his anger is fitting. If he were to be happy instead, that would not fit—unless he really hated that television and was happy someone finally took it off his hands. We normally do not think happiness fits wrongdoing. Rather, we think that happiness fits happy happenings. This is why it would be awkward or disconcerting to see a person get happy at cruelty in the world. Instead, we expect some emotion or attitude geared toward acknowledging the cruelty and doing something to change it when you can. To take another example, we might expect Maria to be angry that her dog was mistreated by someone she trusted. We have these expectations because we think that a fitting emotional response to cruelty is anger, not happiness.

Lordean rage is a fitting response to racial injustice. It fits the occurrence called racism—in all its many forms. It makes sense to feel Lordean rage toward racial wrongdoing. When Bob feels Lordean rage because Native American voters are being disenfranchised in his community, his rage is fitting. When Maria has Lordean rage in response to the racial profiling of immigrants, her rage is fitting. It would be unsurprising to discover that Bob and Maria are angry.

We should not only be concerned with fittingness but also with the appropriateness of anger. Some philosophers think there is no distinction between fittingness and appropriateness.[8] As they see things, for an emotion to be fitting it must also be *morally* appropriate. For example, a person might argue that envy—at least the garden-variety kind—is not a fitting emotion in response to what others have and you lack and therefore desire, because it is not morally right to want others to lose something so that you can have it. But as philosophers Justin D'Arms and Daniel Jacobson explain, this might not be correct. They describe such thinking as committing the *moralistic fallacy*. As they point out, "An emotion can be fitting despite being wrong to feel."[9] I am persuaded by their view. While some critics think that feeling anger is bad and therefore unfitting in any circumstance, I think that we should not move so quickly. My envy can be fitting although morally inappropriate. I may respond to a lottery winner's fortune with envy. Although it is morally wrong to wish that they lose their fortune, it is fitting to respond to their luck with envy. Similarly, my amusement can be fitting while being morally inappropriate (e.g., when a joke is plain *funny*, however wrong it may be). So what are the conditions for (fitting) Lordean rage to be appropriate?

Lordean rage can be *morally* appropriate when it respects the humanity of the wrongdoer and aims to create a better world rather than tear the wrongdoer down in the name of virtue signaling, for example. In other words, if you are feeling rage against injustice and you aim that rage in a way that is productive and in good faith, rather than just at making a provocative statement to portray yourself in a certain light—righteous, fearless, politically active, and so on—that rage is morally appropriate. Lordean rage becomes morally inappropriate when the features of rogue or narcissistic rage (which we saw in Chapter 1) begin to seep into it. That is to say, Lordean rage becomes morally inappropriate when it becomes directed at scapegoats or aims to eliminate the other. This form of rage can be prudentially appropriate when it is metabolized rather than suppressed—that is, channeled toward action—or used to defend the humanity of oneself or others. It can be inappropriate when it consumes one's life, causing a person to neglect matters that are also important to them.

But this is not the end of the story. We should also ask, do fit and morally and prudential apt anger correctly represent the world?[10] If it is the case that Maria's dog was not mistreated, then we would say that although her anger was fitting, it misrepresented the world. In other words, the thing she felt rage in response to, or claimed to feel rage in response to, did not actually happen. She mistakenly thought her dog was mistreated by her friend. If Bob misheard a "Go back to your own country" comment, then his anger—although fitting—misrepresented the world.[11]

Representation matters here because "representing" is one of the things that emotions do in the world. "Emotions involve evaluative presentations," argue D'Arms and Jacobson. "They purport to be perceptions of such [things] as the funny, the shameful, the fearsome."[12] In other words, certain emotions should present to us things like "funny" or "scary." Fear represents the fearful. Shame represents the shameful. What does Lordean rage represent?[13] It represents things like "racism," "racial injustice," or "unfairness." Lordean rage is fitting when it is in response to something racially unjust or insulting—and when something is indeed racially unjust or insulting, it correctly represents the world.

More on "Getting It Right"

A person is always correct in thinking that Lordean rage is a fitting response to racism, but this does not mean that she will always be right that a particular event is a case of racism. People do get things wrong. We would have to judge the rage on a case-by-case basis to see if that case of rage is correctly representing wrongdoing. In the particular context of anti-racist anger, we can start by giving those who are enraged the benefit of the doubt, given the deep history of racism.

Anger can track an injustice correctly, but incorrectly credit that injustice to the wrong person.[14] For example, if a man calls Maria a bitch for being critical in a meeting at work but has never criticized his male colleagues for being just as critical in the past, Maria will be right to be angry at the misogynist coworker who has called her this terrible name. Maria would be wrong, though, if she was angry not just at that man but at every other man in her company—or every man, period. As we see in this example, fitting anger can be either mixed or fully correct. Rogue and wipe rage are examples of mixed cases. As we saw earlier, wipe rage tracks an injustice but incorrectly attributes the injustice to the wrong people. However—unlike these varieties—Lordean rage, at least ideally, is fully and unequivocally justifiable because it correctly tracks the violation (racism) and wrongdoers (their racist attitudes, actions, etc.).

To say that this rage always tracks racial injustice would be going too far. We can safely say this instead: Lordean rage is *more likely* to correctly represent racial injustice than rogue, wipe, and narcissistic rage. Why? Because we live in a racist world. The frequency of the wrongdoing that gives rise to Lordean rage—instances of racism of all types—as well as the rigid requirements for uptake that often follow it makes it more likely that this particular type of rage represents the world.

As the student protest examples show, Lordean rage—which arises in a social context of persistent racial oppression and injustice—is likely not to come about because of one isolated incident. Those with Lordean rage do not see their experiences of racism as isolated or as rare occurrences—nor should they. The instances of racism—whether they be actions, statements, or policies—which lead to and inspire righteous rage of this kind are systemic and thus frequent. They are part of the air we breathe and are deeply embedded in the world through which we move. The anger expressed at Yale or Mizzou was anger bubbling to the surface that had been present for a while. Even though a particular incident often prompts an expression of emotion, emotions are often responses to a pattern of events over time. You react to individual instances sometimes, but other times, the very accumulation of the emotion takes a toll of its own, and you feel annoyed or fed up by the frequent events that cause you to feel the same, bad way again and again. Lordean rage is no exception. This is not to say that people cannot be irritated by a racial wrongdoing done to them. But we get angry in a Lordean way at repeated forms of racial wrongdoing or at systemically reinforced racial wrongdoing, and we find the reasons why in the very features of the rage.

As we know, Lordean rage is distinctive not just because it responds to racism but because its aim is to bring about change—and radical change at that. It aims at nothing less than transforming our world. Someone who experiences one single incident of racism won't always feel the full force of that world-changing rage toward justice. It's not required that they do so, in any moral sense. More likely, a person will feel something more like narcissistic rage in response to isolated incidents. In particular, if a person experiencing a single instance of racism does not see how his situation is connected to other people's experiences of the same wrongdoing, they, by definition, will not feel Lordean rage as a result. If the rage they feel is aimed at change, it's on a more local scale: their rage is saying, "Stop messing with me," rather than, "Let's change the world so it doesn't allow this kind of racism again!"

It bears repeating that the perspective that informs Lordean rage comes from Lorde's most famous statement: "I am not free while any [one] is unfree."[15] And because these words are so important and so true, even if someone is experiencing racism for the first time, he can respond with Lordean rage if he sees his first-time experience of racial profiling, for example, as a frequent occurrence for people who look like him, people who as a result are still not free. He is unlikely to feel merely inconvenienced but more likely to be filled with Lordean rage because he has become a target of a frequent racist event, although he is experiencing it personally for the first time.

The student protests happened due to an accumulation of slights and legitimate grievances. There were racial slurs, repeated neglect, several hate crimes, and a culture of racial insensitivity. These racial incidents were not isolated. They happened frequently, and this frequency not only brought about the rage but made it time to respond with a rage that was aimed at something bigger than these local events. Frequency helped confirm, for those involved, that racism was really happening in the world.

If I see a flash on a screen once and then it disappears, I can chalk it up to a case of "just seeing things," which means that I didn't really see anything at all. Perhaps my mind was playing tricks on me; that can happen sometimes. But if I keep seeing flashes, I can be *more confident* that it actually is happening, that I am likely correct in my observation. The frequency helps confirm the truth of my assessment. So it is with racism. The frequency with which racial incidents occur confirms that I am right in thinking that racism exists. A person might object by noting that conspiracy theorists see confirmation of their conspiracy theories everywhere. What then is the difference between conspiracy theorists and those with Lordean rage? Lordean rage involves some *knowledge* of racism, just as love involves some knowledge of the object of its affection. In this way it is different from other emotions deeply felt by conspiracy theorists like anxiety and uncertainty—emotions that are more likely to lead to *inaccurate confirmations*.[16] In other words, when you experience racism, you don't just *think* that's what has happened—you know it. Now, maybe—especially if you are someone who has not experienced racism firsthand—you need some convincing to believe this is true, but we'll look at precisely how this works.

Just as the frequency of exposure to something may improve our epistemic viewpoint—the perspective through which you *know* things—it can also corrode it. For example, it can desensitize us to features to which we used to be sensitive. Or it can hypersensitize us to features that are not all that important. In the case of racism, then, being subject to racism again and again could make you know it when you see it, or you might worry, following this line of thought, that it may make you think racism is coming at you at all times, even when it isn't. What reason do we have for thinking the effect of frequency on anti-racist anger will improve rather than undermine a person's epistemic viewpoint—that is, the viewpoint from which people gather information that allows them to know things for certain?

Frequency can improve one's epistemic viewpoint in the following sense: if there's a criterion for R, racism, event E may occur but happen so fast, subtly, or when I am not paying attention that I am not able to see if E matches the criteria for R. But if E_1, E_2, and E_3 occur, I have more of a sample size and more opportunities to see if their features match onto criteria for R. If they do, I can say that the frequency helps me be more confident about the phenomenon and in the chances that my emotions, in response to it, are correctly representing it.

This way of understanding how the frequency of a type of experience can help us assess it may not *always* guarantee success, but often it can be helpful. Consider the history of sexual harassment in the workplace. Women had felt that they were victims of mistreatment before there was a name for it. Those women began to hear about the experiences of other women. Together, their experiences began to match some phenomenon that fit the criteria of a form of gender mistreatment; the frequency helped them all understand the source of their discomfort, and it made them feel that their discomfort was representing something real in the world. It was no longer something that was in their heads or an illusion brought about because they did not have thick enough skin.

It's possible that in some instances maybe they got it wrong, interpreting something as sexual harassment when it was not (although, admittedly, given the volume and variety of the stories that emerged particularly thanks to the #MeToo movement, these are hard to imagine). If such a thing happened, you could have an emotion that did not represent what happened in the world. In general, there are plenty of instances when people experience something and do not assess it correctly—one example might be men who believe they did nothing wrong when they in fact sexually harassed women. If they felt rage at being wrongfully accused, this would misrepresent the world, as it would not be based on what actually happened. Of course, there are many instances in which people misinterpret events when processing their experiences. We all experience the world through our own subjectivity—there is no getting past that fact. But the frequency of a certain type of experience at least helped in the case of women who experienced sexual harassment, and similarly it helps in instances of racism.

If a person unused to experiencing racism—someone who does not have the (perverse) benefit of experiencing it often—does face one instance of racism they may say, "I thought I was just being sensitive," because "that was just an accident, not a big deal." However, if it keeps occurring (and one sees that it is satisfying criteria R) a person can be more confident that racism and discrimination are happening and that the anger is correctly representing this racism. Racism in the United States is frequent. This can be easy to miss, though, if one defines racism in explicit, specific, systematic terms, looking for instances as obvious as Nazi persecution of the Jews in the Holocaust. But racism functions not only through specific positive plans for genocide or other similar forms of evil discriminatory action but also in sneaky little ways: through indifference, for example. Not only does racism occur frequently in the present, but current racist acts are continuations of historical racist ones—sometimes in different clothes, other times in the same old threads.

If this is not convincing enough, let's consider another reason why Lordean rage is more likely to correctly represent racism than rogue, ressentiment, narcissistic, and wipe rage. In a white supremacist society, three obstacles tend to keep people from believing that what others—typically people of color—claim is racism actually is racism: white ignorance (willful ignorance of injustice), white skepticism (discrediting accounts of racism by those who report having experienced it), and white empathy (oversympathy for whites).[17] Call these the *three obstacles to uptake* because they make it difficult for Lordean rage to be taken seriously. However, these obstacles—themselves injustices—explain why anti-racist anger is more likely to correctly represent racism than the other types. The reasons follow.

The outraged often run up against white ignorance when they express their Lordean rage at racism. *White ignorance*, a term coined by political philosopher Charles Mills, is an active unwillingness to know, or willingness to ignore the facts about our racial reality.[18] This includes white-washing, myth-making, and victim-blaming: practices used to distort reality. White-washing includes sanitizing the actions of whites at the risk of distorting the truth. To do this requires myth-making: the creation of stories and images to justify white innocence and explain away racist actions. Victim-blaming exonerates the misdeeds of whites by placing the blame for racial wrongdoing on racial minorities instead of holding whites accountable. White ignorance is "the refusal to perceive systemic discrimination, the convenient amnesia about the past and its legacy in the present."[19] We see white ignorance in the Yale lecturer's Halloween email. She saw white students' actions as provocative and not offensive. She saw them as reflecting playful, contemporary times and not part of a history of racism.

Similar to white ignorance is *white skepticism*, a hostility to and resistance of testimonies of racial injustice, particularly by Blacks, Indigenous folk, and People of Color.[20] Disbelief and doubt are the default positions of the skeptic. In order to be convinced, white skepticism demands overwhelming evidence. To accept the truth of a hate crime, a skeptic needs to see the videotape. After watching the videotape, he needs to see the whole video because "context matters." After hearing testimony about racial discrimination from a South Asian American, a skeptic may need to hear from a white person in order to corroborate the previous testimony, or the skeptic may decide to consult a social science study instead. Now, one might think that all of this is an admirable sort of epistemic caution, given the seriousness of the charges. But the problem with white skeptics is not their skepticism, per se. It is the selectiveness of their skepticism. They apply different epistemic standards to claims made about one racial group than they do to those made about another. They would have no problem believing another white person at their word. The standards of proof required to believe something shift, making white skepticism quite inconsistent. The white skeptic is hiding racial bias behind the veil of epistemic responsibility.

While those with white ignorance and skepticism do not easily see racism, or are not easily convinced of such, they may tend to see whites in the best light, always giving them and only them the benefit of the doubt.[21] If they do, then they have *white empathy*. Those with white empathy are empathetic by default to the *motives* of whites (he didn't mean it), the *tone* of whites (he was just joking), the *agency* of whites (he's just twenty years old), and the *freedom* of whites (recall "give them room to be a little bit inappropriate" in the beginning of this chapter).[22] The logic is quite similar to what Kate Manne describes as "himpathy"—our excessive empathy for the rich and powerful, especially men.[23] In order to illustrate how himpathy operates, Manne describes the himpathy we extend to men who are perpetrators of sexual assault. While Manne admits that capacities and qualities like sympathy and empathy are important, "they can also have a downside, when all else is not equal: for example, when social inequality remains widespread." She continues, "Their naive deployment will tend to further privilege those already unjustly privileged over others. And this may come at the expense of unfairly impugning, blaming, shaming, further endangering, and erasing the less privileged among their victims."[24] She specifically sees this naive deployment and further privileging in the 2016 Brock Turner rape case. The Black Brock Turners of the world do not get treated so well. Those who extend white empathy are not empathetic to the plight of marginalized groups—groups that are unfortunately victims of those with whom they empathize. Extending white empathy comes at the cost of mistrusting witnesses, minimizing racial wrongdoing, and gaslighting others, to name a few of its many negative impacts.[25]

Given the three obstacles (in addition to the white supremacy that gives rise to them), Lordean rage is met with demands for overwhelming evidence in order to be heard or understood.[26] We hold Lordean rage to an extremely high standard, in other words. This is an evidentiary burden. One might even say that it is an example of what Miranda Fricker describes as an *epistemic injustice*—"a wrong done to someone in their capacity as a knower."[27] But it is also a piece of a triple burden. Call it the *triple emotional burden of oppression*. This triple burden occurs when members of racially oppressed groups experience injustice, carry the anger in response to it, and then work hard to convince others that they have a right to be angry.

Consider the triple emotional burden of oppression in the following examples. You, a Black person, are hassled by the cops for no reason (other than racial profiling), and as a result you spend all day at work angry, and later when you express that anger to a friend, he starts brushing off your feelings and making excuses for the cops. We also see it in the case of the angry student protests. Students were targeted with racial slurs, carried around anger in response to this mistreatment, and then wrote messages online and protested on campus to convince the school and the public that they had a right to be angry. It's not a single blow—it's a relentless pummeling with each new incident. (And meanwhile, the wrongdoers just walk away and get on with life.) This triple burden is psychologically and physiologically taxing.

One possible upside to the evidentiary burden is that the high standards for Lordean rage to be taken seriously challenge the outraged to build their case even more strongly. This does not mean that they will always have strong evidence, or that they will be heard. But it does mean that their rage—due to constant encounters with the three obstacles to uptake—is more likely to correctly represent racism than the other anger variations. And it has to, in order to have any chance of being taken seriously. We can contrast this to cases in which the anger of powerful white men is often immediately taken seriously—without much evidence—due to their social position. Also, other kinds of rage don't have encounters of the same kind with the three obstacles as Lordean rage does, even if those who feel those other kinds still face challenges from white ignorance. This is because of the target of Lordean rage: those who perpetuate and are complicit in racism. People with Lordean rage do not have to assume that the target of their rage must take one highly specific form. This is quite different from wipe rage, whose target is scapegoats, and narcissistic rage, whose target is only those who target the angry person.

Let's say you are still not convinced that anti-racist anger is more likely to correctly represent racism than the other anger varieties. Well, the only thing left is to point to the facts. Racism, racial inequality, and racial violence exist, undeniably. Hate-crime violence in the United States hit a sixteen-year high in 2018.[28] During the COVID-19 outbreak, there was a surge in Asian Americans reporting racially motivated hate crimes.[29] The racial wealth gap continues to widen—with the typical white family making eight times more than the typical Black family.[30] The forty-fifth president of the United States, for a long time, refused to denounce white supremacist and white nationalist organizations, groups that were also explicitly in support of his presidency. When moderator Chris Wallace gave the president an opportunity to condemn them in the first presidential debate of 2020, he strangely replied that they should "stand back and stand by."[31] Present-day police shootings with impunity exemplify contemporary state violence against Blacks. Videos flood the internet showing individual acts of racial aggression—the killings of Ahmaud Arbery and George Floyd being the most prominent examples—in which people of color are treated in ways that would be unthinkable toward whites. Even if the examples aren't as extreme as actual police killings, nonwhites are brutalized in countless other ways every day: called racial slurs, kicked out of businesses, told to speak English, and reminded of their membership in an underclass that dates back to slavery and colonization. These are the facts. And these facts give us reason to take Lordean rage seriously, in comparison to other kinds of rage at perceived racial injustices, because these other kinds of anger (i.e., wipe and rogue rage) are limited and don't necessarily cover all these examples of racism at work. If we can take for granted that something about racism is systemic (as we surely can), then Lordean rage is the kind that is well suited to know and address that system well, while the other kinds of anger that I've described jump to conclusions about the causes and nature of relevant problems.

However, despite this evidence being in plain sight—in real life and across the internet on which we spend so much of our time—white ignorance, skepticism, and empathy remain. In a recent NBC poll, 89 percent of Blacks reported that discrimination against Blacks is a major problem, while only 68 percent of whites did. Eighty-four percent of Blacks reported that whites enjoy societal benefits that Blacks do not, while only 47 percent of whites did.[32] There's evidence of racism *and* also evidence of social trends that deny, downplay, and prevent uptake. The triple burden continues.

This may not change any time soon, but in the meantime, any rage that is in response to the evidence just presented is correct (at least *minimally*) in its representation of the wrongdoing. It is possible that a person's Lordean rage can represent racism as more or less pervasive, more or less persistent, or more or less pernicious than it really is—particularly if the person experiencing the rage has a disposition to exaggerate or downplay events. I say "minimally correct" for a reason. This is not to say that this representation is perfectly accurate, but perfect accuracy shouldn't be the bar that rage has to clear in order to be a correct representation of the world.

Does Intensity Matter?

Representation deals with the target and correctness of rage. Fit describes the relationship between the occurance and the rage. Philosophers describe these two things as the *shape* of emotions. But an emotion can also be appropriate in the sense of its *size*—meaning its level, intensity, and proportionality relative to what it is responding to. Talking about the size of rage helps us figure out whether its level and intensity are proportionate to the circumstances. (We might also refer to size as "scope" or "force.") And if it is proportionate, we might therefore conclude that the anger is appropriate.

So how can we assess rage based on these types of criteria? One option is that we can put it through a kind of Goldilocks test. Is the rage in question an overreaction, underreaction, or just right when it comes to its intensity? I admit that in the case of Lordean rage I am skeptical of such a test, for reasons that shall be made clear.

We could think that sometimes Lordean rage is too large for the circumstances—it is simply not proportionate to the racial injustice that inspired it. For example, we might think that feeling an intense level of anger in response to one person calling someone else the N-word is appropriate, but it may be too large if the first person referred to the second person as "you people" instead. Now, this may be hard to judge. (For one thing, someone can say some words that are offensive, but not wildly so, but in a tone so full of hatred that it evokes a much stronger response in the target of those words—for good reason.) If a microaggression makes a person irate rather than simply disappointed or briefly annoyed, we may say that is an over-reaction. (Of course, what qualifies as a microaggression, as opposed to something much worse, is itself subjective.) But it's hard to judge if having a strong response to a microaggression would actually be an overreaction. It could be one microaggression after an accumulation of others, and the accumulation could give someone good reason to feel rage that is large in its level and intensity.

We have to be mindful of this possibility when we assess how people respond to seemingly small instances of racism. People tend to assume that an episode of anger is a response to a local event but often it's actually a response to a pattern of events. For example, microaggressions are not isolated episodes of innocent stereotypes. They are recurring slights that have subtle racialized meanings. Derald Wing Sue, a psychologist who popularized the term around 2010 (after the pioneering work of Chester Pierce), defines *microaggressions* as "brief and commonplace daily verbal, behavioral, and environmental indignities, whether intentional or unintentional, that communicate hostile, derogatory, or negative racial, gender, sexual orientation, and religious slights and insults to the target person or group."[33] What may seem like an overreaction to someone saying, "You people," may actually be a "just right" reaction to its subtle meanings: "You are part of the other" and "You are not like us." Similarly, what may seem like an overreaction to the "compliments"—"You have good hair," or "You are articulate for an Asian person"—could be a "just right" reaction to their subtle meanings: "Black hair is not aesthetically pleasing," and "Asians do not speak English well."

And these subtle meanings have real-world effects. Chester Pierce, the Harvard professor who coined the term "microaggression" in 1970, explains, "Most offensive actions are not gross or crippling. They are subtle and stunning. . . . Even though any single negotiation of offense can in justice be considered of itself to be relatively innocuous, the cumulative effect to the victim and to the victimizer is of an unimaginable magnitude."[34] What effects might microaggressions have on those at whom they are aimed? They can make their targets feel alienated and induce imposter syndrome. They can also cause race-based trauma. A 2018 study conducted by Carrie Hemmings and Amanda Evans and published in the *Journal of Multicultural Counseling and Development* found that 89 percent of clients who had symptoms of race-based trauma named "covert acts of racism" as a contributing factor. Given these subtle meanings and effects, anger directed at microaggressions should not be so easily dismissed as an overreaction. It is also worth noting that the angry reaction is not only to the microaggression but the larger systemic problems it represents, and the long-standing, prevalent prejudices that it refers to, even in, as Pierce says, "subtle and stunning" ways.[35]

In feeling Lordean rage, we could think that we could also underreact to our circumstances. Our rage could be too small for the situation at hand, and therefore inappropriate. We might think that if a person is angry at being called the N-word, but not *extremely* angry, then that person underreacted. And we might think, rightfully, that this low degree of anger indicates that the anger is defective in some way. We shouldn't be so quick to deem this type of anger an underreaction, though. Since racism in the United States is persistent, victims of racism always have reason to be angry. Given this reality, victims of racism may temper their anger, if only a little, for reasons of self-care. In this way, it may *seem* to someone on the outside as if the intensity of the anger does not match the event—although the person still feels the anger deep inside. The person may have decided not to allow the anger to become so intense as to affect their peace of mind or day-to-day life. But this is not to say that the person holds no anger toward racism. So rather than saying that a person who has a relatively mild response to racism, even a relatively minor, (regrettably) ordinary instance of it, isn't angry enough, we should allow for the fact that they are just feeling rage at a level that is balanced and that works for them in the long term. As they probably know, this isn't the first time nor is it likely to be the last time they will have to deal with this kind of offense, or something even worse. While comparatively low in intensity, their anger is a balanced emotional response. They are playing the long game, trying to get through another day in a racist world.

There may also be a threshold effect. What may seem like a disproportionate response to something minor could just be someone finally breaking under a pressure that has been building for long before that single incident, which is easy enough for us to understand. But the inverse is also true: if a person is constantly reading about racial violence in the newspaper, their angry response to the tenth

event may not be as intense as the previous nine. This does not necessarily mean that they have become desensitized to racial wrongdoing, causing them to underreact to racial violence. It could mean
that the tenth event did not cause them to feel *more* anger over time
or experience more bodily responses (e.g., increased heart rate) in
an intense way. But this does not mean that they underreacted in
their rage.

We could also react "just right." And if we do, our anger could be
said to be proportionate and at the appropriate level of intensity relative to what inspired it. But we should question this as well. Seneca
wrote, "If you want the wise man to be as angry as the atrocity of
men's crimes require, he must not merely be angry, but must go mad
with rage."[36] And this would count as acting just right: feeling a rage
that is in proportion to the wrongdoing in question. In the context
of racial injustice, the wrongdoing is so grand and intense that, for
anger to fit its size, it might be grander than any of us is ready for—
greater than many of us may be ready to acknowledge is indeed "just
right." An actually just-right level of anger would involve feelings
and even perhaps displays of anger that we probably do not really
want. And as we've discussed, we don't want to *require* people to respond with a rage that intense. Doing so would be asking too much
of the angry and oppressed.

In addition, the intensity of our anger is affected by so many
factors outside of our control that to base anger's appropriateness on
intensity would be unfair. Factors that can affect Lordean rage's size
include differences in people's temperament, culture norms related
to scope, intensity of our emotional lives, and even the weather. For
this reason, philosopher Nicolas Bommarito recommends that instead of focusing on proportionality to determine if the anger is virtuous, we should instead focus on if the person's anger is showing a
proper amount of concern for what is right.[37]

While Bommarito's interesting argument is concerned with what
matters to our moral character, that is not my focus in this book.
For Bommarito, proportionality between the concern that's at the
heart of the anger and the situation is what makes the anger virtuous. Bommarito moves our thinking in the right direction by

divorcing the intensity of anger from standards of appropriateness and introducing more relevant features.

Lordean rage basically is, by definition, rooted in moral concern—it's about caring for racial justice and how people are treated. In general, it is likely to be fitting and correct, given the evidence we have about patterns of racist behavior. That means that even if the rage is disproportionate—either too big or too small—it's still morally important. If we're looking for a good test for whether or not rage is apt, intensity is not it.

The Value of It All

Although we have just spilled a good bit of ink on the fit, appropriateness, and correctness of Lordean rage, let's be clear: anti-racist anger is not important just because it gets reality right. Truth for truth's sake may give us a reason to want to have appropriate anger, but that reason is not why fit and apt Lordean rage is morally and politically valuable, and it is not why Lordean rage plays an important role in anti-racist struggle. So we have to ask: what important claims does fitting, apt, and correct anger make in a racist context?

Appreciating Justice and Recognizing Injustice

Lordean rage not only registers racial injustice. It recognizes and advertises justice's worth.

A person can recognize injustice without experiencing anger. We all know that just because the Dalai Lama resists anger, that doesn't mean he doesn't recognize wrongdoing. Fitting and apt anger is a way of registering injustice, but it is not the only way. Amia Srinivasan, in her essay "The Aptness of Anger," refers to the registering of injustice as appreciating injustice. As she reminds us, appreciating and knowing are two different things. Appreciating injustice through anger has a distinct value, separate from knowing that there is an injustice, just as appreciating the beautiful and sublime has a value that is distinct from knowing that something is beautiful and sublime. If a person recognizes injustice but is cold or feels nothing in response to it, perhaps "there is something missing in her . . . that it would be better . . . if she were capable of feeling anger towards the injustice she knows to exist."[38] Now, no analogies are perfect and Srinivasan is aware of this. And though there is a difference between feeling cold, feeling nothing, and feeling the way the Dali Lama may feel—registering injustice albeit without feeling the anger that, for many others, comes from this registering of injustice—I think we can agree with Srinivasan's "missing point" even if we cannot make sense of what exactly is missing.

Lordean rage is a way of appreciating racial justice in the sense of recognizing its worth. Just as anger registers injustice, it also expresses that there is a better choice, a better alternative. Apt Lordean rage appreciates racial justice by recognizing it when it is not there. Apt Lordean rage also appreciates racial justice by wanting it where it is absent and by desiring more of it whenever it appears in inadequate doses. Remember that the aim of Lordean rage is change. Change is what those with anti-racist anger work toward. They wouldn't want to strive for it unless they believed it was *worth* having. In being angry at that which we want to overthrow (injustice), rage points to something that is worth having. While the *demand* for change calls for justice, rage—whose aim is change—advertises justice's worth. It says that justice is worth having—especially when we channel anger into action to work toward that goal of justice.

This point is very important to establish, particularly in a context in which many are either satisfied with the racial status quo or do not want to disrupt it. It is also important in a context in which many do not think that racial justice is worth their time and attention, or worth fighting for. Lordean rage says that despite the moral apathy, ignorance, and bigotry of others, a better world is worth desiring, imagining, creating, and fighting for. Racism and practices of racial inequality may be worth preserving for some, depending on their goals. Preserving the racial status quo may allow some people to create and maintain self-esteem, by not questioning deep-seated attitudes or worldviews—like a worldview based on white supremacy, profiting off of the racial misfortunes of others, or continuing social and cultural dominance—or continuing to not only believe but assert that white supremacy is and should be the world order. Lordean rage declares that racial justice is worth the fight against the formidable racial status quo—and it is worth it because it helps bring about a more just, equitable, and free world for everyone.

In our current political climate, certain risks come with having a Lordean rage that declares that racial justice is worth the struggle. One of those risks is being dismissed as a social justice warrior. Although the term "social justice" is over two hundred years old, its pejorative usage is quite recent. Some conservatives think that calls for social justice are inappropriate since, according to their thinking, life's difficulties are mostly due to individual choices and failures, not lack of social equality. Demands for social justice are also viewed as inappropriate calls to make everyone equal, when in fact it is impossible for people to be equal in every way. As a result, for these conservative critics, racial justice—as an issue that falls under the banner of social justice—is not worth the struggle, and those who think it is are misguided warriors engaged in an illiberal fight. Another risk of displaying Lordean rage is to be mistreated by the same people whose actions you are protesting. So when an angry person peacefully protests police brutality, brutalization by officers patrolling the demonstrations can still occur against them. Nevertheless, those whose rage is fitting and appropriate take the risk of being dismissed and mistreated in this way. Announcing and reminding the world that racial justice is worth it may have a personal cost. But for some, the risk of negative consequences is worth the price of announcing the worth of racial justice.

When student protestors at Mizzou decided to go on a hunger strike or delay their participation on the football team, they were signaling that justice was worth something. When the Black students at Yale posted their reports of racism online, they, at the risk of being gaslighted or blacklisted, were saying justice was worth it. When Portland protestors in 2020 continued to protest racism—despite the intervention of federal agents—they were appreciating justice. When NBA and WNBA players decided to briefly boycott their games in response to the shooting of Jacob Blake in Kenosha, Wisconsin, and then demanded that their sport organizations join them in denouncing racial injustice, they were appreciating justice. When Black Formula One world champion Lewis Hamilton decided to wear a T-shirt saying, "Arrest the cops that killed Breonna Taylor" and "End Racism," before and after a Grand Prix race—despite possible consequences from the International Automobile Federation (FIA)—he was appreciating justice. This appreciation was not merely evident in the sacrifices the students, protestors, and athletes made, but in the anger that informed their actions. They were saying that no matter the cost, justice was worth it. Their fitting and apt Lordean rage was a way of registering injustice *and* a way of recognizing the importance and desirability of justice.

Pointing Out Disvalue, Pointing to Value

Fitting and apt Lordean rage points out racism in all its forms—including but not restricted to structural, invisible, and new racisms. It also marks the value of racially oppressed people.

Another source of the power that fitting and appropriate Lordean rage holds comes from the way it brings attention to moral problems. Rage gives us a way to bring attention to the fact that something has gone horribly wrong. This marking is important especially regarding racism, since many people still think that racism is a thing of the past. For example, while Blacks are more likely to report that the United States has *not* achieved racial progress, whites report the opposite—and whites reach their conclusions by comparing current times to the past.[39] In their view, racism is a historical event that is no longer part of our present. Racism is US chattel slavery; the bombing of four little girls in a church in Birmingham, Alabama; the racial terror of the Ku Klux Klan; or the proliferation of "Whites Only" signs in the Jim Crow South. Since those events occurred in the past and are no more, racism no longer exists. When evidence of racial injustice, such as the racial wealth gap, is presented, some prefer to explain it away by relying on ideologies such as meritoc-racy; nonwhites should simply try harder and work harder if they want to catch up with whites.

Lordean rage marks these current manifestations of racism. It says that racism has not disappeared as some might think. It alerts us to the very fact that racism is still part of our present. The angry protests that have recently captured our attention—most notably beginning after the tragic murder of Black teenager Trayvon Martin by a neigh-borhood watchman in 2012 and unfortunately still ongoing—seek to shine light on the fact that racial problems in the United States are deep and still very much a reality.

Lordean rage also marks new racisms. Some people think that racism is no more because they fail to consider the ways in which racism changes over time. Racism adapts and appears not as ex-plicitly as it did in previous decades. Scholar Martin Barker has identified these *new racisms*:

> Today "new racism" practices have emerged that are more sophisticated and subtle than those of the Jim Crow era. . . . These practices are as ef-fective as the old ones in maintaining the racial status quo. . . . Black-white racial inequality is produced and reproduced in the United States in four areas: social, political, social control, and economic.[40]

We can see new racisms in what happened at Yale. While Yale students were angry that swastikas were found, they were also angry about "racially insensitive" Halloween customs and an email sent by an educator asking that students have space to be "provocative and inappropriate." Both instances are practices used to maintain the ra-cial status quo, although they are more subtle than racial epithets, for example. The students' Lordean rage sought to mark this new racism. This is not to say that "old" types of racism have disappeared. Lynchings, gerrymandering, and disenfranchisement are unfortu-nately not a thing of the past. Subtle and explicit practices of racism coexist.

When some white people do recognize that white supremacy is part of our present, not just our past, they often individualize it.

White supremacy is thought to be what the alt-right personifies, what radical groups endorse and perpetuate, not ordinary citizens or the structures and systems that surround us. And radical groups or "a few bad apples" (as violent police are often called) do not, in the predominant (white) view, represent what America is. However, this view of racism, white supremacy, and racial injustice as events perpetuated by a few, in limited instances, is misguided. White supremacy is not an isolated event. It is a structure. It is an "overarching political, economic, and social system of domination."[41] Lordean rage helps to mark this structure for those who might not otherwise perceive it. While it is easy to merely point to the racial misdeeds of a few students on campus, Mizzou students' Lordean rage did not stop there. Through it, they sought to bring attention to an unjust structure that was embedded in the education institution, not just an isolated thing that happened on their campus.

Lastly, Lordean rage marks "invisible" racism. People who uphold racist structures prefer that they not be discussed. Silence is preferred, and the reasons for it are myriad. Many whites and even some racial minorities benefit from a racist system. While they might deny that they are racist, they may still prefer not to bring attention to a system that privileges them based on race. They may even struggle, even to the point of taking up arms, to maintain their privilege. However, Lordean rage marks what some prefer to remain hidden and what others are ready to defend by any means necessary.

Both the Yale and Mizzou students' anti-racist anger marked explicit racial wrongdoing and the silence of both universities' administrations. Yale students' rage pointed to the unjust attempt at privileging the offensive expression of one group over the dignity and safety of others. It declared that Yale had allowed a culture to exist on campus where people would think this behavior was acceptable.

Lordean rage not only points to this disvalue but it also publicly marks value—because anger is a way of responding to value. When we value someone or something, it gives us reason to respond with anger at their mistreatment or the threat of it. Since "our evaluative stance toward each other is constituted to a significant extent by the way we are disposed to feel," Lordean rage is a way to respond to people, ideas, and relationships that we value.[42] It marks this value in the world. Although I say more in Chapter 4 about the connection between anger, respect, and value, this point is worth exploring now, if only briefly. When we respect (as a mode of valuing) someone as a person, we are saying that they have the authority to make certain claims on us and hold us accountable when we do not meet them (for example, through blame or indignation when we disrespect them). But part of this respect is recognizing that third parties should also meet the same claims, and that we hold them accountable when they do not. When people we value and thus respect are wronged by third parties, Lordean rage publicly marks their value by holding others accountable for the wrongdoing. Lordean rage not only points out that wrongdoing has occurred but also that victims of the wrong-doing are persons of moral worth and moral status.

The rage of the student protestors publicly marked what they valued. Their anger showed that they valued Black students and had respect for them. It showed that they valued a university that is in-clusive and makes students feel safe. Their rage also showed that they valued the physical and psychological safety of members of their col-lege community. Their actions, inspired by Lordean rage, asserted that, as the popular movement's name says, Black lives matter.

If the apt Lordean rage of protestors was in response to the mis-treatment of those whom they valued (Black students), their anger publicly marked that value. In marking that value, the anger expressed value for the mistreated group. If the rage of protestors was in response to the mistreatment of those whom they valued (this time, all students on campus), their anger would have pub-licly marked that value. In marking that value, the anger would have expressed value for the mistreated group. But since Black students at Yale and Mizzou, and not all students, were being mistreated, it made sense to focus on the group on whose behalf their anger was provoked. It was not that the students thought that all lives did not matter. Their anger was a specific marking of a certain group that was being mistreated. Even without the slogan, their rage would have marked that value. The slogan only gave voice to a rage that was already communicating and responding to value. This point also applies to the wider phenomenon of protestors chanting, "Black Lives Matter," as they protest.

* * *

Gaslighting is a tool of manipulation employed to make those who have anti-racist anger question and doubt their experiences, judgments, and thus their emotions in response to racism. As shown at the beginning of this chapter, making someone's anger about something else is gaslighters' go-to strategy. The aim, particularly for racial gaslighters, is to try to make anti-racist rage about something other than racism (for example, saying it's not about injustice but freedom of speech, civility, or honoring of the flag, in the familiar example of former NFL player Colin Kaepernick). That's one way to undermine the anger. But then once that's done, the gaslighting truly begins. Once the subject has been changed, the gaslighter can tell the angry person (and others who observe them) that they are crazy because their anger doesn't make sense, given the description of it.

Gaslighters do this in order to make the outraged doubt the existence of racism and to prove anger's unfittingness and inappropriateness, all with the hopes of quieting the rage. And gaslighters do this not merely to silence the noise but to prevent the communication of value of the oppressed, the reality of racial wrongdoing, and the need for justice. But we must not fall into the gaslighters' trap.

Lordean rage—anger against racism that aims toward real change—can be fitting, appropriate, and correct. We cannot let those who wish to silence anti-racist anger be the ones who get to evaluate it, whether it's based on aptness, fittingness, intensity, or anything else. They don't get to make the rules, since they are invested in undermining the very thing that rage seeks to accomplish, highlight, and change.

In making my case for Lordean rage, I hope that I have succeeded in laying out some guides to assist in such an assessment, but remember that such an assessment has to be made in good faith. The upshot of what I've laid out here is not in anti-racist anger passing the assessment test, though. Appropriate Lordean rage plays an important role in anti-racist struggle in that it points out racial injustice, declares that racial justice is worth it, marks disvalue, and publicly highlights the value of racially oppressed people. But as we will see, Lordean rage can do even more.

3
Rage in Work Clothes

People often make a distinction between being angry and behaving angrily, telling you that there is nothing morally wrong with *being* angry. The problem lies in *behaving* angrily—acting on the feeling of anger.[1] Behaving angrily is often made synonymous with *behaving badly*. The angry person behaves badly by burning down buildings, screaming at the top of their lungs, and slashing people with their ruthless words. So while nothing is wrong with feeling rage, anger, and fury as long as you keep them to yourself, the problem is that doing so isn't easy. These feelings have the power to ignite dangerous behavior. Along this line of thinking, maybe we'd be better off not having these feelings in the first place? After all, angry behavior is seldom productive behavior.

I admit, I have seen people act out in rage, and it has not always been pretty. All the way back in ancient Rome, Seneca also witnessed this kind of rage—in his case, among those in political power. It was such an ugly picture that he described anger as "consist[ing] wholly in action and the impulse of grief, raging with an utterly inhuman lust for arms, blood and tortures, careless of itself provided it hurts another, rushing upon the very point of the sword, and greedy for revenge even when it drags the avenger to ruin with itself."[2] This was anger so out of control it had even lost track of its purpose and its true target. Pure rage. Commenting further on this ugly kind of anger, Seneca continues,

> No plague has cost the human race more dear: you will see slaughterings and poisonings, accusations and counter-accusations, sacking of cities, ruin of whole peoples, the persons of princes sold into slavery by auction, torches applied to roofs, and fires not merely confined within city-walls but making whole tracts of country glow with hostile flame.[3]

Perhaps we too have witnessed or experienced what Seneca did—people behaving badly when angry, people losing control. But before we fully accept Seneca's account and indictment of angry behavior, we must be mindful of the kind of anger he is describing. He is not talking about Lordean rage. Instead, he is alluding to the wrath of powerful rulers who were motivated by greed and dismissive of the lives of those who served and lived under their command. Different kinds of anger fuel different kinds of action. The action need not be necessarily bad.

Anger of the kind we have been calling "Lordean rage" can fuel positive action directed toward ending racial injustice and creating an anti-racist world. Some of us may have already experienced first-hand the motivational pull of anger in our lives. Perhaps we can recall a time when our anger made us work harder or provided the motivation to prove to those who once discounted us that they were wrong.[4] But how does this happen exactly? In the context of racial struggle, *how* does Lordean rage motivate us to fight for justice? Given anti-racist rage's power to fuel the fight for justice, should we still be trying to replace it with more "positive" emotions? In other words, why exactly should we give rage a chance? In order to address these important questions, first we should look at what other thinkers have said about the connection between anger and positive action, particularly yet more broadly the link between anger and the pursuit of justice.

Anger and Justice

Making connections between anger and positive action is not an inventive intellectual move of the modern era. Ancient Greek philosopher Aristotle and eighteenth-century British philosopher Joseph Butler made connections between anger and justice long before philosophers like me were born, noting particularly anger's uses for preventing injustice and pursuing justice.

Aristotle thought that anger was useful for preventing injustice as well as its perpetuation. How is this possible? Well, anger is communicative. One of the first things we do when we act on anger is express it. One way to express it is to declare to others that we are angry. When we express anger we communicate to others that a wrongdoing has occurred and that someone is to blame for that wrongdoing; likely, although not always, the person to blame is the target of the expression. (We've all been in the position, of course, of lashing out at some poor person who just happens to be there with us when we are mad at someone else.) When we express our anger, we communicate that there will be consequences for wrongdoing. Those consequences might begin and end at just having to endure our expression of rage—which can be big or small, made of words alone or words and vengeful actions.

We don't have to lash out in epic rants or violent actions to express rage in a way that communicates to wrongdoers. Evolutionary biologists have observed that we are wired to pick up on even just angry facial expressions, so that we can perceive when someone's face is telling us, "Stop, or else!" Anger functions as a deterrent for future wrongdoers as well. We are less likely to harm a person if we know there will be consequences for our actions. These features of anger help explain how anger can be useful for preventing unjust actions.

But anger's ability to communicate with wrongdoers—before and after the wrong has been done—is not the only way that anger prevents injustice. As Aristotle explains, a person who is angry at an insult is more likely to defend himself and is less likely to endure being insulted—both good things. (Whether the angry person then defends himself in a violent or nonviolent way is a question for another time.) The actions of defending oneself and others and refusing to be insulted preserve the dignity and lives of people. They are, therefore, positive actions. We can then say that you can take anger and aim at a positive goal: the defense of oneself (and others) and the refusal to be insulted. Those who are not angry, by Aristotle's account, are not only less likely to engage in these positive actions, but they are fools.

Those very things that Aristotle thinks you can aim at through anger are core to resisting racial injustice. An angry person, for example, is likely to defend a friend or stranger who is told to "speak English" by a customer in a store aisle. An angry person is likely to defend themselves when they encounter dehumanizing practices and policies. However, it still matters how you go about achieving what you aim for, even if it's a positive aim.

Joseph Butler, whose writings on anger and forgiveness are influential, discusses anger's connection to justice more specifically. In two of his sermons delivered to a packed audience at a London Church, Butler rejects the idea that anger, in general, helps us pursue justice; that's because he makes a distinction between sudden and settled anger. (He is a member of the *type distinction camp* that I discuss in Chapter 1.) Sudden anger is excessive and misguided—think of acting while your feelings are still hot. Settled anger, on the other hand, is not—it is the anger you feel when you've had a chance to process your thoughts and collect yourself. Moreover, settled anger's object is moral evil. This type of anger aims at justice instead of revenge and is compatible with goodwill. For this reason, Butler thinks settled anger helps us rectify and end unjust, evil acts. He writes,

> The natural object or occasion of settled resentment then, being injury, as distinct from pain or loss, it is easy to see, that to prevent and to remedy such injury, and the miseries arising from it, is the end for which this passion was implanted in man. It is to be considered as a weapon put into our hands by nature, against injury, injustice, and cruelty.[5]

Aristotle almost gets to a place of saying anger helps fight injustice but stops short. But centuries later, Butler gets us there.

Butler also claims that settled anger has a motivational component that helps us use it as a weapon in our justice pursuits.

> And after an injury is done and there is a necessity that the offender should be brought to justice; the cool consideration of reason, that the security and peace of society requires examples of justice should be made, might indeed be sufficient to procure laws to be enacted, and sentence passed: but is it that cool reflection in the injured person, which, for the most part, brings the offender to justice? Or is it not resentment

and indignation against the injury and the author of it? I am afraid there is no doubt which is commonly the case.[6]

What Butler says could be read simply as an observation of what *tends to happen*: "after an injury is done," people tend to require a motivation beyond reason, like emotions, in order for them to act. Or they require a more passionate motivation like anger rather than cool reason in order to act. But it's possible that Butler isn't just saying how things tend to go. With the rhetorical questions he poses, he may be leading his audience to realize the error of their ways and try to act differently in the future. Rather than falling into the easy trap of thinking that calm reason alone can get us everything we want, we have to consider the role of anger. Either way you interpret what Butler is saying here, one point is clear: anger provides the motivation to fight against injustice.

We don't need to reach so far back in history to see good arguments for using anger to fuel positive action. More recently, feminist scholars have moved the conversation forward by specifically talking about how anger can help drive progress in issues of feminism, racial equality, and the important intersection of the two. Unsurprisingly, one of the most influential claims in the feminist literature on this topic comes from Audre Lorde: "Anger between peers births change, not destruction, and the discomfort and sense of loss it often causes is not fatal, but a sign of growth."[7] For Lorde, anger can motivate social progress and transformation, and if there is a cost to achieving change through anger, it is worth it.

In her 2018 book *Eloquent Rage,* scholar Brittney Cooper recognizes, like Lorde, that while Black women's anger is not always productive—particularly when it is turned against themselves—it can be used for productive ends. She writes, "When we turn it outward and focus it on the power that would crush us into submission and give back to us a mangled image of ourselves, Black women's rage is a kind of power that America would do well to heed if it wants to finally live up to its stated democratic aims."[8] Journalist Rebecca Traister echoes this idea, affirming that "women's anger spurs creativity and drives innovation in politics and social change, and it

always has."[9] As Traister reminds us, historical movements of abolition, suffrage, and labor came about because of the anger of women
like suffragist Maria Stewart and abolitionist Ernestine Rose. In her
2018 book *Good and Mad,* Traister talks with women candidates,
activists, and #metoo accusers who reveal their desire "to take anger
and transform it into something else."[10] Traister attributes the large
number of women running for seats in the House of Representatives
(a total of 309 in 2018) to their anger brought about by the 2016
presidential election. She cites Luiba Grechen Shirley, a congress-
woman who entered politics after 2016 and was also able to petition
the Federal Election Commission to use campaign funds to pay for
childcare, as crediting anger at various injustices for her entrance
into politics. "I was enraged," she says. But Traister also notes that
women's anger has not only motivated activism but also radical art
ranging from Ntozake Shange's play *For Colored Girls Who Have
Considered Suicide / When the Rainbow Is Enuf* to Naomi Alderman's
novel *The Power,* to the feminist street art of Tatyana Fazlalizadeh.
These are all examples of what Traister describes as "furious female
energy" and she credits anger as its major source.[11]

   As you can see, alongside ancient criticisms of and warnings
against angry, destructive actions lies a long history of claims about
anger's ability to fuel positive action. However, while claims have
been made about the power of anger to motivate political action,
scholars, writers, and activists have not explored *why* this is the case.
That is, how is political anger like anti-racist rage able to fuel positive
action?

   To try to answer these questions, we can look at empirical research
on eagerness, self-belief, and optimism—the fuel found in Lordean
rage that motivates anti-racist struggle. When we put this research
together with other normative arguments, like the ones we've seen
that establish that anger fuels positive action, we can begin to understand why Lordean rage works—and why it's *not* the case that such
rage is counterproductive, or that it should be replaced with more
supposedly positive emotions.

   With this foundation we are able to appreciate the psychological
role that Lordean rage plays in helping motivate people to disrupt

and dismantle racism and unjust policies. We also can understand the complex and even complementary relationship Lordean rage has with the emotions we are often inclined to recommend as its replacement.

The Fuel

If we say that Lordean rage provides the fuel to motivate people to engage in anti-racist struggle, what does that mean? What is really going on when this fueling happens? It helps to consider the specific components that help make the concept work so well.

Eagerness

Researchers have found that anger, unlike fear, elicits approach tendencies—a propensity to move toward an object rather than away from it. This happens specifically when we feel anger in response to goal frustration, goal pursuit, and the attainments of rewards.[12] Racial justice is an example of such a goal or reward.

When anger arises, then, a person who has a goal—like racial justice—is likely to be eager to act.[13] And it is the approach motivational aspect of anger that readies the individual to act in order to change the situation or remove its morally problematic components rather than run away from it. Audre Lorde was right. When we feel our goal of racial justice being frustrated, and experience anger in response to that, the object of our anger is change.[14] We can see this all happening when we look at the brain.

Numerous studies in psychology and cognitive science locate anger in a specific region of the brain that is related to approach. Activation in the left frontal region of our brains is known to show an approach state, while activation in the right frontal region of our brains shows an avoidance state. For example, researchers created situations to induce either an avoidance or approach state in participants by inciting certain emotions.[15] They used electroencephalograph machines to record where the high brain activity was occurring. First, to incite an avoidance state, they showed participants repellant films or presented them with punishments. When they did, researchers recognized that participants showed elevations of the right hemispheric activity associated with an avoidance state. However, when they presented participants with situations in which there were rewards, they noticed higher levels of left activation in participants' brains. This activation showed an approach state.

We might think that negative emotions correlate with an avoidance state and positive emotions, an approach state. By positive emotions I mean emotions that tend to have a pleasant feeling and a positive judgment of its stimuli. Negative emotions have an unpleasant feeling and a negative evaluation of its stimuli. But when a person experiences anger (an assumed negative emotion), if the aim of that anger is a goal or reward, it activates high levels of activity in the left frontal parts of our brains, making us highly motivated to go after that goal.[16]

Lordean rage, as a subclass of anger, has this approach-related effect. Although Lordean rage negatively evaluates wrongdoers and may not feel good when experienced, since it has a goal (e.g., racial justice), it makes the person with Lordean rage eager to do something about the situation—eager to approach rather than avoid it. And this eagerness effect has its benefits. When fighting against systemic problems such as racism, the task can be overwhelming. Systemic problems are powerful, often facilitated by powerful people. When the powerless decide to take on systemic problems, the task can seem too great; a person may feel too small, and that may provide reasons not to even try at all. But a person with Lordean rage is empowered by the motivation it provides to not retreat but to go forward to transform the situation. The power she is against may, in instances of fear, lead her to avoid challenging systems. However, the approach motivation that comes as a result of Lordean rage can lead her to approach her goal and obstacle. It makes her eager rather than discouraged to act.

Being eager to act is also important because changing any oppressive system is hard work. When the going gets tough, it's easy to quit. But a person who is motivated to fight is more likely to keep pursing her goal. This is also helpful in contexts of ongoing oppression. Racism is not a new phenomenon. It has a long history and is very much ongoing. When racial discrimination, mistreatment, and oppression are ongoing, a person needs fuel to keep fighting. Lordean rage, with its eagerness to approach its target and reach its goal, provides this fuel.

Optimism and Self-Belief

Anti-racist rage, as a subclass of anger, not only makes us eager to act to change the situation. It also impacts our attitudes. Studies have shown that anger makes people optimistic about future events.[17] It also has this optimistic effect because anger influences our perceptions of control and certainty.[18] To that end, angry people think that good things are going to happen and that they will prevail regardless of what happens.[19] The reason is that anger triggers a bias into thinking that the self—the angry person—is powerful and capable. Interestingly, Aristotle alluded to this anger and optimism relationship thousands of years ago when he wrote, "For since nobody aims at what he thinks he cannot attain, the angry man is aiming at what he can attain, and the belief that you will attain your aim is pleasant."[20]

Optimism is important in the pursuit of racial justice. There may be instances in which you are fighting but are unable to see any sign of progress or change. In some instances, your efforts might achieve change; other times, not. Moral progress is not linear. It ebbs and flows. There could be moral progress one year and a rollback or backlash of progress the very next. (The election of Trump, a person who had engaged in racist behavior for decades, after the first Black president, Obama, seems to be an obvious example here.) It can be hard to be optimistic in such times. But the upshot of Lordean rage is that it can make a person believe that he can still effect change even when all the evidence is against him. To engage in any fight, whether in a boxing ring or political campaign, you must believe in yourself. The belief that you can influence the situation—no matter how small, Black, or poor you are, or how many other intersecting, marginalized identities you may occupy—is important in any campaign aimed at transformation.

The optimism that is influenced by rage is not just restricted to attitudes and beliefs about yourself and your situation. Anger is also associated with optimistic perceptions of future risks.[21] In other words, those who are angry—compared to those who are fearful—are more prone to make risk-seeking choices, and these choices are influenced by people's beliefs about themselves. Angry people's optimistic beliefs influence the risks they are willing to take.

I can understand this firsthand. Usually when I am angry due to goal frustration in my professional life, for example, those moments highly motivate me to do something particular about my situation.[22] In response, I often take risks that I normally would not take if I was not angry. I often seek out opportunities that I would normally not seek out due to fear, lack of belief, or procrastination. And I do it knowing the risks involved (e.g., being rejected, putting myself out there). But my anger, in distinct ways, makes me want to risk it all, so to speak. We can imagine the ways this can go wrong. I could take unwise risks—and no doubt people often do, given this level of optimism. (We talk about such risk-taking more and how to safeguard this from happening in Chapter 6.)

This fuel metaphor—made up of eagerness, self-belief, and optimism—helps explain the motivational role that Lordean rage has in anti-racist struggle. However, a person may still have a worry. If Lordean rage, as a subclass of anger, has this fuel, so do wipe, narcissistic, rogue, and ressentiment rage. What is then unique about this fuel as it relates to Lordean rage? Focus on that question misses the point. It's not that Lordean rage offers a distinct kind of fuel. Rather, what's special about Lordean rage is that it has the power to lead to distinct (positive) action. Revisiting the features of Lordean rage, as well as other kinds of anger that arise in response to racial injustice, can help make this clearer.

As we have seen, Lordean rage is a response to racism. It is not a response to "all white people" or to anyone who steps in the way of the outraged. The aim of Lordean rage is to bring about change—to create a world in which racial injustice is no more. Its action tendency is to metabolize it—that is, to make it useful for certain ends. The perspective that informs Lordean rage is not a selfish or hateful one; rather, it entails the notion that "I am not free until we all are free." Given these features, we can begin to see how such rage can provide the fuel of eagerness, self-belief, and optimism that is necessary for positive action rather than the negative actions that so worried Seneca.

If one's anger has an inclusive feature that focuses on justice for all and does not see any one person as an enemy, it is likely to fuel or motivate action that is directed at a lust for peace and equality rather than action that is (for Seneca) "raging with an utterly inhuman lust for arms." If the object or goal is change and a just world, an angry person is likely to be greedy for a better social and political system—a world we can all live in together rather than being "greedy for revenge." If the anger's aim is to bring about radical change, it is likely to fuel action that seeks to end all slave systems rather than see "the persons of princes sold into slavery by auction." And those who have this anger are likely to be eager to engage in these positive actions, optimistic about such engagement, and confident of their success. The anger I am describing that can do these things is Lordean rage.

However, if one's anger focuses exclusively on destruction or sees everyone as the enemy, it is likely to provide an eagerness, self-belief, and optimism that will fuel or motivate *negative* action. A person with wipe rage is likely to make risk-seeking choices to accomplish the goal of elimination. A person with narcissistic rage is likely to believe that they can change the situation—a situation that only affects and thus benefits them, but not other oppressed people. A person with rogue rage is likely to think that good things will happen for him but not for others, and may engage in destructive acts to help produce that outcome. None of these problems occur with Lordean rage; unlike rogue, narcissistic, and wipe rage, Lordean rage lets us avoid these issues. This point is important for understanding *how* Lordean rage helps the outraged engage in anti-racist struggle.

"Focused with precision, [Lordean rage] can become a powerful source of energy serving progress and change."[23] This rage has the energetic potential to inspire and spark action directed toward what Lorde calls "a basic and radical alteration in all those assumptions underlining our lives" rather than "a simple switch of positions . . . [the] ability to smile or feel good."[24] Things don't always go according to plan. Lordean rage can become useless when it fails to fuel positive action. While it often fuels positive change, it doesn't always succeed in doing so. (In Chapter 6 I provide anger management techniques—inspired by Lorde and others—to help ensure that Lordean rage achieves its goal.) But for now, it's simply important to see all the ways in which Lordean rage has a deep, unique potential to inspire us to take positive action. Then it's up to us to use it in the fight for what is right.

Fueling Freedom Fighters

The connection between Lordean rage and the fuel components I have described may help explain the positive actions of people we admire—people who stood up to racially oppressive systems. I have always wondered what made freedom fighters like Sojourner Truth and Ida B. Wells stand up to oppressive racist and sexist systems. They were doubly oppressed—and had double odds stacked against them, being both women *and* Black—both being born as slaves and living through some of the darkest years in terms of treatment of Blacks in America. But despite it all—having seen firsthand how unjust America could be—these women fought for racial justice and were not afraid to speak truth to power. What accounts for this audacity? No doubt, it was a belief in justice. But it seems likely that they were also driven by a belief in themselves and the future, and an optimism that they would be able to succeed despite the risks and challenges they faced. I suspect that one of the primary sources of such confidence and optimism was what I have been referring to as Lordean rage.

Truth's famous "Ain't I a Woman" speech is an indignant oratorical masterpiece in which she demands equality and proclaims her humanity in front of white folks who did not want her to speak to them in the first place. While standing before women suffragists as well as white male hecklers at the 1851 Ohio Woman's Rights Convention, Truth proclaimed,

> That man over there says that women need to be helped into carriages, and lifted over ditches, and to have the best place everywhere. Nobody ever helps me into carriages, or over mud-puddles, or gives me any best place! And ain't I a woman? Look at me! Look at my arm! I have ploughed and planted, and gathered into barns, and no man could head me! And ain't I a woman? I could work as much and eat as much as a man—when I could get it—and bear the lash as well! And ain't I a woman? I have borne thirteen children, and seen most all sold off to slavery, and when I cried out with my mother's grief, none but Jesus heard me! And ain't I a woman?[25]

A *New York Daily Times* reporter described Truth as being undeterred by the insults and as "raising her hand and voice in wrath." She spoke with so much anger and force that the reporter asked readers to "imagine Trinity church organ . . . with its low bass and trumpet stops pulled out, all the keys pulled down, and two men and a boy working for dear life at the bellows, and you have a gentle specimen of the angry voice of Sojourner Truth."[26] This was not the voice of "the cool consideration of reason" as Butler would say, but a fresh, hot, and righteous rage, aimed at seeking justice. Her boldness, audacity, and self-confidence exemplify Lordean rage at its finest. Truth would continue to use that rage to fuel her abolition and desegregation work.

Likewise, for Ida B. Wells, Lordean rage provided fuel in the fight for justice—in her case specifically driving her to crusade against racial violence in the form of lynching. Through her journalistic work,

Wells helped bring attention to white mob violence, and she continued fighting for racial justice even after a white mob burned down the office of her newspaper, the *Memphis Free Speech and Headlight,* and drove her out of Memphis, and eventually to Chicago.

Wells historian Patricia A. Schechter, in her 2001 intellectual biography, points out the angry tone of Wells's antilynching writing and highlights how Audre Lorde's account of anger describes Wells's life work.[27] Schechter writes,

> The determined quality of Wells's prayers and the "dynamitic," angry tone of her journalism deserve further comment. Wells's anger distinguishes her visionary standpoint from the calculus of business and politics characteristic of her secularizing age. African American poet Audre Lorde reminds us that anger is "loaded with information and energy" crucial for survival, even as racists and other opponents use its expression to discredit, dismiss, or punish black women. "Anger is a grief of distortions between peers," Lorde explains, "and its object is change." Such was the thrust of Wells's visionary pragmatism. Wells raised pointed, often angry questions about racism and inequality in the United States. She demanded practical answers to questions posed in the spirit of Isaiah and Jeremiah, biblical prophets whose exhortations sometimes began with a sardonic "Ha!" Like the prophets' passion for Zion, Wells's visionary pragmatism was shaped by a righteous rage that was also part of the work of love.[28]

Since it is not a secret that Wells was angry, it is safe to infer that anger influenced her beliefs and the risks she was willing to take to fight against racial violence. You cannot be a Black woman in the nineteenth century, write inflammatory work, challenge the status quo, and not believe in yourself and the risks you are taking. And what helps explain Truth's and Wells's ability to do so? Lordean rage. A person who has this anger will tend to think of herself as capable of bringing about an anti-racist world, will take certain risks, and will believe that those risks are worth taking in order to achieve her goals. We see this in the lives of Truth and Wells—powerful, optimistic, and angry women.

When Rage Gets in the Way of Positive Action

Of course, you might be thinking, what if you are not Truth or Wells? Does Lordean rage always lead to success and acts of historic bravery? Can such rage ever get in the way of positive change, rather than inspiring people to fight for it? If it could, this would be a serious cause for concern, so it's worth investigating these important questions.

To be systematic in exploring this issue, we can examine some of the main ways a person might try to say Lordean rage is counterproductive. These are not *all* the ways people may try to make this point, to be clear, but they are the ways that deserve to be taken seriously, because, if true, they would provide overriding reasons—reasons that trump other ones—to not make a case for rage.

Deterring Potential Allies

You might think that even if a person has Lordean rage that can fuel positive action, the very presence of that rage may still deter potential allies from joining with them in fighting for racial justice. In this way, the rage can be counterproductive. Since making social progress on a grand scale may require not only the marginalized's participation but also that of the privileged or those who are *more* privileged than the oppressed (and social movement history provides many such examples), it is wise to recruit allies as opposed to deter them. There are several reasons that a person might think that Lordean rage can deter potential allies while also fueling positive action.

The first reason has to do with empathy. Philosopher Adam Smith, who is most known for *The Wealth of Nations*, was a moral philosopher who provided an extensive account of empathy in his first book, *The Theory of Moral Sentiments*, written in 1759. In the text, Smith offers arguments for why we are more and less likely to empathize with different kinds of people. He also gives accounts of the role that empathy plays in admiration and the approval of anger, among other things. When we observe someone expressing anger toward someone else, Smith suggests that we are likely *first* to empathize with the person with whom the person is angry, and then with the angry person. The reason is that we understand the fear and potential danger felt by the person who is the target of the anger much more quickly than we know if the angry person's anger is appropriate or not. In saying this, Smith gives us some insight into why people may worry that Lordean rage might scare off potential allies. When a potential ally sees someone expressing Lordean rage, they may be less likely to empathize with them first, and more likely to empathize with the target of the other person's anger. There is a risk that the potential ally may stay there—refusing or unable to do the work required to understand the angry person's point of view. This might not be the case if the anger wasn't there at the outset.

So is it right to say that Lordean rage is counterproductive in that it alienates potential allies? No, and here's why: this failure of the potential ally to empathize with the person expressing rage isn't a problem with the rage itself—it's a problem with the potential ally. Note that Smith says that we are *first* likely to empathize with the person with whom the person is angry and then the angry person. But empathy with the angry person is possible. The potential ally's refusal to empathize, by stopping at the target of the anger, is not Lordean rage's fault. It is due to the ally's inability to do the work required to understand the person's rage—work that might include imagining himself in their shoes and gaining the necessary information about the angry person and the racial situation in order to assess both from the position of what Smith calls the "impartial spectator."

Another reason that a person might think that anger alienates potential allies has to do with the idea that when people are angry, they appear irrational and out of control to others. The thinking goes, if a person is read as irrational, it is difficult to see how she can rationally convince another person of injustice and the need to fight against it. Under this view, the most persuasive way to convince people of something is through a calm presentation. Calmness, then, is equated with rationality. Lordean rage is not.

Although Seneca believed that an outraged person appears like a madman, some philosophers have worked hard to disconnect anger from irrationality. For example, Butler describes sudden anger as being of the irrational type, but he also claims that settled anger is very much rational and he recommends it. But let's address the worry more specifically. Is it the case that the best method of persuasion is through a calm, rational presentation as opposed to an angry one? While this question is empirical, something can be said from the armchair.

To answer this question, I think it's important to make a distinction between (stereotypical) angry behavior and angry speech. Angry behavior, like the conduct Seneca describes angry rulers as displaying ("slaughterings and poisonings"), is indeed less likely to convince a moral person to become an ally for justice. It is not only irrational and far from calm, but destructive. However, those with Lordean rage do not necessarily engage in *this kind* of angry behavior—behavior that is more likely to occur in cases of rogue and wipe rage. If it does occur in Lordean rage, then it is a case of morally inappropriate rage and we have reasons to criticize it.

Is the worry about calm presentation connected to angry speech? In other words, does anger expressed publicly through speech deter potential allies? This depends on its expression. Incoherent, threatening, and out-of-control speech is unlikely to convince moral and rational people. But this can be said about speech in general—not just angry speech. Angry speech is not by definition irrational and out of control. More importantly, there are instances in which angry speech is likely to persuade potential allies to join the side of the oppressed. This is possible when angry speech, according to political philosopher Maxime Lepoutre, "help[s] [potential allies] imaginatively experience what it is like to be in the speaker's shoes, how the world appears or feels from where they stand."[29]

Black abolitionist Frederick Douglass is an exemplar of such angry speech, and he was able to use it to win over potential allies. To encourage, as oppose to deter, potential allies, Douglass delivered fiery speeches to arouse empathy in his audience so that they could feel his anger and understand why they must join him in fighting the target of his anger—slavery. Historian James Oakes describes how, when Douglass spoke, "he roared, his booming baritone complemented by waving arms." Those in the audience for these speeches could "feel—viscerally—the bloody horrors of slavery."[30] Douglass's oratory enriched his audiences' understanding of slavery and persuaded other abolitionists like William Lloyd Garrison to join him in the fight. Garrison would later write, "I shall never forget . . . the extraordinary emotion it excited in my own mind—the powerful impression it created upon a crowded auditory. . . . I think I never hated slavery so intensely as at that moment; certainly my perception of the enormous outrage which is inflicted by it . . . was rendered far more clear than ever."[31] Angry speech can have the effect of recruiting allies—as opposed to deterring them—by inspiring anger that helps them recognize and understand racial injustice. Calm presentations may be persuasive, but presentations that express and even excite Lordean rage can also be persuasive, and therefore useful for recruiting, as opposed to deterring, potential allies.

The third reason that someone might think that Lordean rage deters potential allies from joining the fight for racial justice is due to fear. Put simply, some worry that Lordean rage can scare away potential allies. People may have experiences with the rage that Seneca was critical of, as well as the wipe and rogue rage that we have examined. These experiences may give them reasons to naturally link aggression and destruction with anger and be wary of it—even the so-called virtuous kind. It's easy to see the source of people's concern, but we have to be careful. There are two types of concerns here: sincere and insincere.

The sincere concern has a general associative nature to it. Anger's link with aggression gives some people immediate concerns, which is understandable, but this shouldn't be the end of the story. One of the things I attempted to do in Chapter 1 was to provide tools to increase a person's emotional intelligence. That is, I offered ways to distinguish anger types that should and should not generate moral concern. I did this in hopes that readers would have the tools to understand different emotional expressions, instead of painting them in broad strokes, and then respond to them accordingly. While a person may be fearful of all angry encounters, such fear is not always

justifiable. One has a choice to use certain tools to try and understand people's emotions on a case-by-case basis.

This new knowledge of various anger types doesn't necessarily
make resisting one's initial fear of anger easier. I am particularly
sympathetic to those whose cognitive ability varies when it comes to
processing other people's emotions as well as those who come from
other cultures (particularly those outside of the angry West who lack
what some describe as WEIRD—Western, educated, industrialized,
rich, and democratic—morality). Different social groups have different thresholds for what counts as an acceptable level or expression
of anger, because some cultures and subcultures are more comfortable with anger than others. In some cases, it may be related to comfort with the passions in general, and in other cases, it may be linked
to attitudes toward anger in particular. As a result, I am aware that
some potential allies are put off by anger for cultural reasons and
not necessarily because they lack emotional intelligence in general.
While they're worth acknowledging, however, these cultural reasons
should not be overriding reasons to not make a case for rage at racial
injustice.

Then there is the insincere kind of concern. The insincere concern
has a *racialized* as opposed to a general associative nature. When
people already hold stereotypes of different racialized groups (consciously or unconsciously) as dangerous, violent, and threatening,
those stereotypes can send all kinds of negative signals to these
potential allies no matter how virtuous the angry presentation. To
give an example, the concept of the "angry Black woman" is such a
deeply entrenched stereotype and cliché that people may dismiss the
statements of a Black woman expressing righteous, Lordean rage as
a result of that stereotype. Given this racialized association, some
people may say the lesson here is that Black women simply should
not express their anger—especially not if they are trying to attract
allies to their cause. But how can that be the solution? Why should
they have to work around the stereotypes projected by others?

Not only is this suggestion fundamentally unfair, it is counterintu-
itive to Lordean rage. Lordean rage has a role to play in dismantling

racism. It does not aim to be complicit in it by encouraging the oppressed to engage in respectability politics for the sake of making people who cannot let go of their prejudices feel comfortable (more on this later). Lordean rage challenges these stereotypes as well as those who hold them. A person with Lordean rage is likely to prefer to issue these challenges rather than give into them. She is also likely to face the prejudices by responding to them with her apt and productive rage.

It's also important to realize that sometimes the message that a person fueled by Lordean rage expresses might itself be hard to take for some potential allies—white people, for example—and it could be the *content* of the message, not the manner in which it is delivered, that deters them from joining the cause. Returning to Audre Lorde is useful here. At the beginning of the essay "Uses of Anger," Lorde recounts a time when she expressed anger at a conference. Afterward, a white woman approached her with a request: "Tell me how you feel but don't say it too harshly or I cannot hear you." Lorde responds to that encounter with a question: "Is it my manner that keeps her from hearing, or the message that her life may change?"[32] Lorde wondered if her angry expression was deterring the white woman from hearing her anti-racist message or was it the anti-racist message itself. This is an important question to ask and an important one to struggle with if you are the one requesting or are tempted to make such a request.

When potential allies express a concern that another person's anger is getting in the way of them hearing, they need to look inward and ask some difficult questions. Is it the message that the Lordean rage communicates (for example, racial injustice is wrong and I must accept the challenge to transform myself in order to transform the world) making me uncomfortable and therefore resistant to the rage? What in the message am I not ready to hear? Is something I am hearing posing a challenge to how I want to think about myself and my role in the racial status quo? Is this other person asking more of me than I am willing to give to fight for justice? If a person says that she cannot become an ally with those who have Lordean rage until the anger disappears, yet it is actually due to her refusal to accept the challenge to transform her life, that person is not yet ready to be an ally—and it is not the rage that has deterred her. Her refusal shows that she is not willing or ready to be an anti-racist. It's possible that a person could ask herself all these questions and decide that indeed it is the harshness of the rage and not the message that is deterring them, but this doesn't settle the issue. They should also ask: Is the harshness related to the intensity? If so, the fact (established in Chapter 2) that intensity is not a relevant standard of assessment in political cases also applies here. Is the harshness of the anger related to angry speech? If so, for the reasons we saw earlier in this chapter, this needs to be rethought—since angry speech on its own can't be to blame. Or is the person disturbed by a lack of civility—for which standards are often moved by and asymmetrical to those in positions of power? If so, that potential ally may not be ready to commit to the cause, since "civility" is often used as a way to control, rather than hear the claims of, the oppressed.

While worrying that Lordean rage will be counterproductive in that it will deter potential allies can be understandable as well as highly suspect, at the end of the day it doesn't represent a major objection to Lordean rage's potential to fuel positive action. Lordean rage will not recruit everyone to engage in the anti-racist struggle. No tactic will. A person should not think he needs to discover the perfect recruitment tool at the expense of giving up a good one like Lordean rage. I do not think any such tool exists. The civil rights movement is an example that even when there is a movement that is based on an explicit nonviolent ethic of love, this does not guarantee that every potential ally will be recruited to the cause. At least I made this point in a 2020 BBC Radio interview about anger. When the broadcaster asked me if I was worried that the actions of BLM protestors in Portland and Kenosha would turn away supporters, I noted that anger is in the business of doing more than recruiting allies. But I also mentioned that no emotion or movement has ever succeeded in getting everyone on their side. It's a high bar to set for anger. More importantly, this high bar obscures the overwhelming support that the 2020 BLM protests were able to garner. Even while angry, there was increased support among white allies at protests. The movement also received overwhelming corporate support from companies like Netflix and Nike to sports organizations like the National Basketball Association and Major League Baseball. The good news is that even while Lordean rage may turn off some potential allies, I've provided reasons for why Lordean rage can still fuel positive action in some allies, even as some potential supporters sit on the sidelines.

Deterring the Powerful

You might think that if a person has Lordean rage, that rage can discourage racial oppressors and those complicit in such oppression from hearing her claims. If the goal is to produce justice in the world, we should be concerned with how we engage with those in power—since they can assist in our pursuit of justice by hearing our claims and, consequently, taking political and social action through law creation and policy reform. There are several reasons why a person might think that Lordean rage can deter the powerful from hearing these claims and thus become counterproductive.

The first reason has to do with defensiveness. Anger can make a person defensive rather than productive. If a person in power senses that, in the message that the person or people feeling Lordean rage are expressing, they are being blamed for the injustice at hand, their defensiveness might get in the way of them changing. Since anger communicates criticism, those in power may be more likely to respond to Lordean rage with defensiveness rather than acceptance. And since this is likely to be the result, it may be wise to address people in power using other methods.

But we shouldn't jump to this conclusion too quickly. It's not clear that their defensiveness is anger's doing alone. Psychological research suggests that what causes defensive responses is criticism—whether angry or not. People usually respond to criticism with defense mechanisms as a way to protect themselves from painful truths or emotions. Achieving racial justice requires bringing about change through combating racial injustice, and you cannot combat racial injustice without calling it out. Criticizing racist individuals, institutions, and structures is crucial. Arguments claiming that we should not criticize when it is warranted because it will not feel good to or be embraced by the criticized do not provide a decisive reason to not criticize at all. This is why Lordean rage is an example of what Brittney Cooper calls "eloquent rage," which is different from "elegant rage." Lordean rage is eloquent because it is articulate: clear in its cause, demands, and claims. But it is by no means elegant or respectable.[33] The goal of people with Lordean rage is not to make their rage look nice or make people feel good. It is not specially crafted to go down easy. This is not to say that people expressing Lordean rage have moral reasons to be cruel, insensitive, and hateful. But importantly, a person with Lordean rage should recognize—and in some cases expect—that their claims can be resisted or denied by those who are blameworthy or under racial stress.

Robin DiAngelo describes whites' defensiveness in response to things like race-based criticism as an example of "white fragility." Because whites never have to deal with race, they become ignorant to its impact and never can admit to themselves the extent of their hand and complicity in racism. As a result, any kind of conversation or criticism will trigger defensiveness. Although she uses fragility to describe whites in this instance, DiAngelo is insistent in not describing white fragility as a weakness. Rather it is "born out of superiority and entitlement. . . . It's a powerful means of white racial control and the protection of white advantage."[34] Instead of putting all the responsibility on the outraged person to not incite defensiveness, those who hear such criticism should learn how to respond to the outraged in healthier ways by taking responsibility, exercising self-compassion, and learning to be anti-racist. Even if a person doesn't respond positively to the criticism, this does not mean that the very act of criticizing was unproductive. The fact that Lordean rage fueled the criticism is an accomplishment and thus a positive action—even if the powers that be refuse to change as a result.

This being said, as important as direct criticism is, I wonder: Is every case of Lordean rage intended to get the attention of a powerful group? And if it fails to get that attention (for reasons having to do with the rage itself), do we have reasons to think that the rage is, all things considered, unproductive? Important work from feminist philosophy can help us try to answer this question.

In her 1983 essay "A Note on Anger," Marilyn Frye compares being angry to a speech act—by which she means that its communicative nature requires that a second party cooperate with it. If I say to Adam, "I promise," but he does not take himself to be someone I am obligated to or someone he can count on, then the promise collapses, since he failed to give my speech uptake. By "uptake," Frye means to take it seriously as a promise. For Frye, anger is similar. Anger makes certain claims. When I am angry at Adam but Adam does not "take the anger on by directly responding to the claims implicit in it," then he does not give my anger uptake. He might resort to calling me crazy instead of angry. For Frye, "Deprived of uptake, [my] anger is left as just a burst of expression of individual feeling. As a social act, an act of communication, it just doesn't happen."[35]

Frye also notes that the anger of certain socially positioned people (like Native Americans or Latinx folk) is likely not to get uptake from others depending on what those others take the concept of "Indigenous" or "Latinx" to be. If I think the concept of "Indigenous" entails inferiority and inequality in relations to Indigenous peoples, I will fail to comprehend their claims with respect and to give their Lordean rage uptake. Contrary to the argument people sometimes make, saying that rage can be counterproductive when it gets in the way of those in power taking up your cause, this is not a reason, according to Frye, not to make such claims through anger. Frye suggests that we can continually express anger, and through that expression we can better understand (through its uptake by others and lack thereof) other people's concepts of who and what we are. Given what Frye claims in the essay, though, this still leaves us with thinking that Lordean rage's only role is to communicate. And if it fails to do this—by discouraging the racially powerful from listening to others' claims, for example—we may have a problem.

Luckily, this is not the end of the story. Lordean rage does not require, in all instances, that the oppressor and those complicit in oppressive behavior be its audience and hear its claims. Philosopher

María Lugones makes a distinction between what she calls "first-order anger" and "second-order anger." First-order anger is communicative. It petitions the powerful. A person expects that this anger would be understood and taken seriously (i.e., receive uptake). Second-order anger, on the other hand, is not seeking uptake. The powerful are not its audience. Second-order anger rejects the norms around what counts as acceptable or righteous anger. "It recognizes this world's walls. It pushes against them rather than mak[ing] claims with them."[36] Lugones's second-order anger is about the inability to communicate experiences of oppression. In Chapter 4, I say more about how Lordean rage can push against the world's walls, particularly a capitalist, white supremacist, patriarchal one, in different ways than what Lugones describes. But here I take from Lugones the idea that Lordean rage does not require that the racially powerful be moved by the anger of anti-racists. In some cases, it is a "noncommunicative act[;] rage cannot be making a claim addressed to those who share the official sense." It decries that racist world that seeks to diminish and distort them, rather than make demands within it. This rage has no "intention to make sense to those within it."[37] This is not to say that one cannot intend both levels of anger (first-order and second-order). But given the possibility that Lordean rage can intend both, it makes less worrisome the concern that rage will deter the powerful from hearing our claims. This is because the rage is not always directed at or present for the powerful in the first place.

Swapping Emotions

Some might worry about Lordean rage for a different set of reasons, altogether different from worries about deterring possible allies or getting in the way of winning over people in power. Some people may worry that, while Lordean rage may work just fine, it might not be the best option on the table, compared to other, more positive emotions. For example, could an emotion like love do the same work, without bearing the moral risks that rage brings with it? Could we do an emotion swap, replacing rage with something softer?

Paraphrasing the Beatles' classic, is it true that all we need is love?

There is a *love myth* that pop psychology, social justice movements, and moral and social philosophy have propagated. The myth consists of the assumptions that love can do no wrong, love is incompatible with blameworthy emotions, and love is all we need in the pursuit of racial justice. Let's look at these assumptions more closely.

First, when people recommend love to replace anger, they end up painting love in broad strokes. They talk about it as though love is always kind, selfless, pure, and a motivator of goodwill. But just as anger is not just one thing, neither is love! Love is not always appropriate and virtuous—even within a political context. If we look at narcissistic rage, we may find love. If we look at wipe rage, we may also find love there. And it is not the virtuous kind that love's supporters think love always is. Rather, we will find an excessive love of self, power, and racial supremacy—and this love can lead people to do indisputably negative things, like protecting themselves at the exclusion of others or aiming to hurt people in various ways—all in the name of racial love.

Say you were to assume that when people recommend that we swap rage for love, they only mean the best kind of love—the kind that avoids all these possible problems. It still isn't necessarily a good recommendation for the simple reason that, by saying rage should be *swapped* for love, it assumes that the two couldn't coexist. It also suggests that love is superior to blameworthy emotions like Lordean rage. And again, even if you assume people are only referring to the best possible kind of virtuous love, we shouldn't take this for granted.

Martha Nussbaum claims that anger conceptually involves payback, and we should replace anger with love and generosity. We should do so, she argues, because love and generosity not only lack a desire for payback, they also lack the moral risks that come with anger. To help us see this love myth in practice, Nussbaum uses revolutionary figures like Martin Luther King Jr. to show that we can still achieve racial justice, for example, without anger.

We tend to credit King for not only leading people to protest injustice and challenge the powers that be but for encouraging love and kindness in the pursuit of racial justice. His life seems to be both an objection and counterargument to my anger / positive action claims since he is not thought of as endorsing anger, but love. Looking over his life and speeches, some scholars argue that his political strategy and speeches were supported by a love ethic, not an angry one. Such a love ethic is what inspired and changed society and pressured political leaders to create just laws and policies such as the Civil Rights Act of 1964. Since King recommended these attitudes and succeeded in his efforts, this provides empirical evidence, according to philosophers like Nussbaum[38] and Glenn Pettigrove,[39] that positive emotions like love and meekness do a better job of fueling positive action than negative emotions like anger.

But King's successes were not the result of love alone. As recent work in religious studies and history has shown, anger played an important role as well. King believed that anger too could fuel positive action.[40]

In her 2018 essay "From Anger to Love: Self-Purification and Political Resistance," Nussbaum seeks to provide a detailed account of King's views on anger. She admits that King doesn't explicitly say much about anger but what he does say gives us some clues about his overall view. I agree. Using the same strategy, I focus on King's life and two passages from his speeches and essays where he references anger. I believe they all support my account of Lordean rage in general, and the relationship between Lordean rage and positive action in particular.

Nussbaum contends that when King admits that anger is acceptable, he is referring to an anger that is without the payback part or that is only a brief episode of anger. Nussbaum takes this to support her overall criticism of anger (that it conceptually involves a desire for payback and status harm) and that an angry person needs to transition out of it (what she calls "transition-anger"). However, reading King, I come away with a different message: King did not have a broad-strokes picture of anger. There was a form of it, unlike the others, that he endorsed: what I have been referring to as

Lordean rage. Such anti-racist anger does not aim for payback or ill-will but change and justice. It is also forward-looking, for it focuses on building a better future rather than enacting revenge for past racial wrongs. But what does King have to say about anger and positive action? His life provides an empirical argument, and his words offer a logical argument for the claim that Lordean rage can fuel positive action.

Clarence Jones, an attorney and speechwriter for King, says that when King was arrested and placed in a Birmingham jail in 1963 Jones read to King a recently published open letter. In the letter, local white clergymen accused King of being an agitator and outsider. The clergymen also urged King to leave the city. Jones recalls, "He [King] was so angry."[41] But this anger did not lead King to punch Jones, resign from the movement, give into the letter's pleas, or seek vengeance on the authors. Instead, King responded by writing his famous "Letter from a Birmingham Jail"—a positive action. In his letter he lays out a case for civil disobedience, challenges white liberals, and expresses an urgent call for justice. It is a brilliant piece of persuasive writing and a classic work in political philosophy.

Among the readers the letter influenced was then-president John F. Kennedy, who made his famous civil rights address on July 11, 1963. Sociologist Jonathan Rieder emphasizes how much of an impact King's "angry" letter had on the president's speech.

> It required the Birmingham civil rights movement—and the tough-minded theory of social change that King spelled out in the "Letter from Birmingham Jail"—to provoke his [Kennedy's] speech into being. And once pushed into taking a stand with the address, Kennedy and his speechwriter Theodore Sorensen filled it with rhetoric often remarkably similar to King's. Though the address came, ostensibly, in response to a different event— the fight over the integration at the University of Alabama—it was full of echoes of "Letter from Birmingham Jail." In a powerful sense, King and the movement were the authors of the president's oratory.[42]

Writing the letter from the Birmingham jail was a positive action that had a positive impact on the country. But let's not forget the emotion that fueled the letter writing—for as Rieder describes, "[The letter] is a Black man's cry of pain, anger and defiance."[43]

As a political philosopher, King employed careful distinctions that also help us to see the relationship between anger and positive action. Note how King describes the anger of the oppressed in his speech "Showdown for Nonviolence":

> I think we have come to the point where there is no longer a choice now between nonviolence and riots. It must be militant, massive nonviolence, or riots. The discontent is so deep, the anger, so ingrained, the despair, the restlessness so wide, that something has to be brought into being to serve as a channel though which these deep emotional feelings, these deep angry feelings, can be funneled. There has to be an outlet, and I see this campaign as a way to transmute the inchoate rage of the ghetto into a constructive and creative channel.[44]

King describes the rage of the ghetto as an inchoate or undeveloped rage. By this, I take him to mean not that the oppressed's rage was new. Rather, it lacked important features like inclusivity, optimism, or aim for change. Absent these features, King was concerned that the rage would manifest into violence, so he expressed the need for the rage of the oppressed to have a creative channel like nonviolent protest. He also thought that the rage could mature through involvement in the civil rights movement. Perhaps through an involvement in a campaign that endorsed certain collective strategies as well as certain attitudes and perspectives, the people involved and thus the rage could transition from wipe or rogue rage and into a rage suited for positive action: Lordean rage.

What were the features of this inchoate rage that differed from the rage that motivated King to write "Letter from a Birmingham Jail"? When we see King criticize anger, very much like James Baldwin (more on him in Chapter 6), he does it when the rage is attached to hate, bitterness, and violence. A person who hates another is not prone to change the situation but to eliminate the other person. Hate leads to negative actions. Militant rage, in King's view, was attached to hate, bitterness, and violence. And for that reason, although he understood it, he could not endorse it.

But the anger that King did endorse was an anti-racist anger that he felt could fuel positive action. In an elegy for W. E. B. Du Bois, King uses Du Bois's life as an exemplar of this kind of anger. He writes,

> History had taught [Du Bois] it is not enough for people to be angry—the supreme task is to organize and unite people so that their anger becomes a transforming force. . . . This life style of Dr. Du Bois is the most important quality this generation of Negroes needs to emulate. The educated Negro who is not really part of us, and the angry militant who fails to organize us, have nothing in common with Dr. Du Bois. He exemplified black power in achievement and he organized black power in action.[45]

Anger alone is not enough to change an oppressive system. As we saw in Chapter 1, certain kinds of anger can get in the way of positive transformation. But a particular kind of anger makes a difference. Militant rage, an anger that has despair and hatred as two of its features, is not likely to ignite the angry person to organize or do anything to change their situation. At worst, it is likely to fuel negative action. Anger can be a transformative force only when it is a certain kind of anger, and that is Lordean rage. Contrary to long-standing opinions about King, he was not against anger of all kinds. His life and work support the view that a particular anger—Lordean rage—can fuel positive action.

To admit this doesn't take anything away from our understanding of King as a champion of love. His anger was not in tension with other "positive" emotions like love. King was still able to express love to his enemies despite his anger at racial injustice. Contrary to the love myth, love is compatible with blameworthy emotions like anger. As I argue in previous work,[46] anger like Lordean rage is compatible with a universal love that involves goodwill and respect (agape love); we can be angry at a loved one for committing a wrongdoing because we love them and are not indifferent to how they fare morally. But the love/anger relationship goes even deeper than this. Anger is not only *compatible* with agape love, but it can also *express* agape love. Lordean rage can express agape love to the hated, the racial hater, and the whole community.

Lordean rage expresses love to the hated in some of the ways that I explain at the end of Chapter 2. Just as Lordean rage can reveal who we value, it can also show that we love them. It expresses this love through our refusal to ignore and let insults directed at others go unchallenged. Lordean rage can also express agape love by offering up criticisms to the racial hater—not only as a means to end their insults toward those whom we love, but as a way to say that we also care for the hater's moral well-being and we care enough to offer up angry criticisms. Baldwin emphasizes this thought through his assertion, "I love America more than any other country in the world, and, exactly for this reason, I insist on the right to criticize her perpetually."[47] Lordean rage can also express agape love to the moral community when it shows that it is willing to stand in defense of and pursue racial justice for the whole moral community, of which we, the hated and the hater, are also a part. Since agape love and Lordean rage are complementary in this way, I do not see why we need to replace love with Lordean rage. Where you see Lordean rage, you are also likely to find agape love. You can use them both in the service of racial justice.

✳ ✳ ✳

We might find virtue in being angry. We might also think that behaving angrily is a vice or simply counterproductive. We are more likely to think this if we also think that angry behavior is always violent behavior. But the insightful work of Lorde, King, Aristotle, and Butler; feminist thinkers such as Cooper, Frye, and Lugones and a host of others helps show that angry behavior might also include preventing injustice, pursuing justice, producing political philosophy, and being helpful to a movement. Angry behavior is not always what Seneca describes. While certain kinds of anger, like rogue rage, fit the vengeful, bloody picture that Seneca paints, another kind of anger does the complete opposite.

Lordean rage can fuel positive action, and it does so because of its aims, perspective, and action tendencies as well as its components of eagerness, self-belief, and optimism. Lordean rage can also fuel positive action because of its complementary relationship with agape love. Lordean rage says, "It's okay to be angry *and* to act angrily." The transformation of our world might depend on both.

4

Breaking Racial Rules through Rage

An image usually comes to mind when we think of the resistance figure who fights against racial injustice. This figure is usually willing to do things like risk their life, speak truth to power, go against the status quo, and engage in or encourage massive protests or rebellions. Figures like Harriet Tubman, Malcolm X, and more recently athlete and activist Colin Kaepernick are paradigmatic examples.

We think that figures like these, who take action, are the only kinds of resistance figures. We might think that if we are angry at racial injustice, we must always *do something* particular with our rage—like rebel or protest—for merely having rage is never enough. And this thought may be assumed to be supported by the arguments we have read about motivation and productivity. Martin Luther King Jr.'s own words might even support the concept; King noted, "It is not enough for people to be angry—the supreme task is to organize and unite people so that their anger becomes a transforming force."[1] With this line of reasoning, just having anger is not enough. You must also do something with it—like boycott or take a knee. We should question this way of thinking, however, in order to appreciate the more varied ways—with Lordean rage—in which people can resist racial injustice, oppression, and domination.

Feminist philosophers have argued that expressing anger is an act of resistance, as is simply experiencing anger. When a woman expresses or experiences anger toward a man, she subverts patriarchal norms and values. She breaks a feeling rule. As Elizabeth Spelman writes,

> To be angry at him is to make myself, at least on this occasion, his judge—
> to have, and to express, a standard against which I assess his conduct. If
> he is in other ways regarded as my superior, when I get angry at him I, at

least on that occasion, am regarding him as no more and no less than my equal.[2]

But the feeling rules aren't just written based on gender. Other rules are written based on race: there are "emotional" lines, for example, that Black people aren't meant to cross; as a result, crossing them would represent an act of resistance, whereas feeling, doing, or saying the same thing would not constitute rule-breaking for a white person. A host of such forms of resistance often go unrecognized, since the transgression that constitutes the resistance is the breaking of an implicit racial rule sometimes so baked into the status quo that it can be hard to appreciate. Breaking the racial rules down helps us better grasp and celebrate these subtler forms of resistance.

Rules and Feelings

Certain social conventions or rules exist about what emotions we should feel in a certain context. You would be surprised to find how many of them you know, follow, teach to others, and enforce on a daily basis. If you were ever told you should feel sad after a breakup, or happy when you get a promotion, you have had firsthand experience with these rules.

Sociologist Arlie Russell Hochschild refers to these social conventions around feelings as *feeling rules*—"guidelines for the assessment of fits and misfits between feeling and situation."[3] When we tease someone for feeling a certain emotion, we are teaching or enforcing feeling rules. We are saying that the person should not have the emotion they have because the feeling does not fit the situation.[4] A person does not have to think that feelings are nothing but social constructions to accept the tenability of feeling rules. (While the social constructionist might say that emotions are, by definition, socially constructed and thus socially enforced, feeling rules only suggest that notions of aptness are taught and enforced in society.)

People who do not follow feeling rules are often viewed as violators. Consider the fictional character Debbie Downer. Before her name became synonymous with a person who dampens the mood of others with her negative words, she was a character in a recurring skit on *Saturday Night Live*. Debbie Downer—no matter the occasion—always finds a way to experience feelings that are in violation of the feeling rules of a particular context. Instead of being excited at Disney World (2004), happy at a wedding (2005), and content at Thanksgiving (2004), Debbie violates feeling rules by expressing fear and worry each time. ("The biggest drawback to working in a theme park must be that you're under constant fear of deadly terrorist attacks!")[5] Worse, she aims to excite these emotions in others. Debbie stands out from others because, skit after skit, she doesn't experience emotions that fit the occasion. The awkward and disappointing responses from members of her social group reveal how uncomfortable she makes them feel.

How did Debbie's friends learn what emotions were fitting for the occasions? Hochschild claims that we often learn feeling rules as children through the instruction of our parents and educators. Even in adulthood we are still learning rules, which are constantly being enforced through social exchanges. We see this when Debbie's friends try to steer the conversation away from, for example, feline AIDS ("It's the number-one killer of domestic cats!") or other topics that tone-deaf Debbie tries to introduce.[6] Feeling rules are not universal; different cultures may have different rules. What someone should be angry about according to China's feeling rules may differ from what someone should be angry about in the United States.

Since Hochschild's contribution, scholars across fields have sought to link feeling rules and power, thereby explaining the variability and asymmetry of feeling rules in different contexts. Philosopher Alison Jaggar describes emotions that break feeling rules as "outlaw" emotions. According to Jaggar, we do not always feel conventional emotions and thus follow feeling rules. This issue is particularly salient with oppressed groups. Their social positioning does not allow them to feel the "prescribed conventional emotion."[7] Jaggar recognizes that "within a . . . white supremacist and male-dominant society," the predominant values in that society will serve the dominant group (rich white men) and "our emotional constitution will be influenced by this."[8] When a person makes a racist joke in this society, the feeling rule will be amusement. When a Black woman experiences misogynoir, the feeling rule will be indifference. When we break these feeling rules by responding to racist jokes and misogynoir with resentment and empathy, respectively, Jaggar claims that we have just responded with an outlaw emotion because it is not what a person should feel within a white supremacist and male-dominant society. Feeling the unprescribed emotion is incompatible with the dominant society's values and perceptions, making it unacceptable in that society.

In more recent work, legal scholar Janine Young Kim makes a more explicit connection between feeling rules and race. Pointing to the racial asymmetry of feeling rules, Kim highlights the ways in which there are different rules (as well as expectations) for different people based on their social positioning. The fact that Black men are expected to suppress their anger when encountering the police, and the idea that slaves were expected to be subservient and happy but not angry, are examples she cites.[9] Elaborating on Kim's account of race and emotions, sociologist Eduardo Bonilla-Silva claims that racial emotions (emotions that race and racism inevitably excite) produce a hierarchical structure of feeling.[10] For example, white women's fear of Black bodies is taken to be a matter of utmost concern while anger at racism is viewed as suspect or not taken seriously.

When the outraged break the feeling rules of a white supremacist and male-dominant society by being angry at racial mistreatment or exploitation (although one ought not to, according to the rule), Kim claims that it is a "form of protest against the shame and meekness that emotion rules attempt to instill among the racialized."[11] While Jaggar labels the anger in this case an outlaw emotion, Kim describes the acceptance and valorization of the anger as an act of "affective transgression." She adds, "[This transgression] is fundamental to th[e] struggle against racism."[12] In order to resist racism, race-based feeling rules must be broken.

In summary, there are feeling rules in a given society that apply to all people in general. However, in a society that is white supremacist and male-dominant, feeling rules for some groups do not apply to others. Based on social positions, the same emotion can be acceptable for some and unacceptable for others. When the outraged person decides to resist these rules by being angry at racism, that anger becomes an outlaw emotion, and by accepting the anger (and violating the rules) the outraged person transgresses against the emotions the dominant society wants and expects them to have. The point is that people not only can violate these rules—it's that they should, and indeed must, if racism is to be resisted.

The work of these thinkers helps us understand the relation between feelings, rules, power, and social positions. However, three questions remain: What specific rules around race can be broken with Lordean rage? How can this be done? And if, as Janine Young Kim claims, the transgression is fundamental to the struggle against racism, how exactly is this the case?

Racial Rules

While feeling rules are clearly part of the picture of when, how, and who gets to feel rage (among other emotions), we must account for the larger role of race as well. We need to account not only for feeling rules but *racial* rules—rules of which feeling rules are a part.

The racial rules I want to focus on are not rules in the sense of Jim Crow laws—the laws in the South from the 1870s to the 1950s that did things like outlawed miscegenation, required segregation of public spaces, and made it nearly impossible for Black people to vote. Unlike Jim Crow, racial rules are not codified in law but socially imposed by individuals and groups.

Racial rules are feeling rules, but they are also behavioral and cognitive rules that people of certain races should follow in a white-supremacist, male-dominated society. Like feeling rules, they are taught to us implicitly and explicitly through social exchanges, the media, the law, and other sources that surround us. The racial rules are enforced through reminders from state authorities, employers, and symbolic rituals, as well as punishments and rewards. These punishments can involve physical death (like the murder of Emmitt

Till for allegedly whistling at a white woman) or social death (like disenfranchisement or censorship). But they can also be enforced in little, day-to-day ways that we might not even register—for example, as we'll see, who can register rage in public without being treated as suspect (spoiler: not Black people). Rewards for following the rules can consist of promotions, acceptances, or safety, to name a few.

Although racial rules include feeling rules, they are not limited to them. Racial rules also involve cognitive aspects (perceptions, beliefs, and values) as well as behavioral aspects (actions and responses) that translate to rules within a given context. However, what we discover here is that these rules are connected to each other in ways that justify their grouping. For example, being angry at racism can break a feeling rule but it also breaks a cognitive rule if the anger involves a judgment that racism is morally wrong and should not be tolerated.

A more detailed account of racial rules also helps us determine the racial rules that affective transgressions and outlaw emotions like Lordean rage are violating, and how as well as why these transgressions are important to the struggle against racism. Although there are a variety of racial rules, two are especially important for us to understand. We'll also see how Lordean rage breaks each of them.

Racial Rule #1: Remember Whiteness and Keep It Holy

In W. E. B. Du Bois's 1920 essay "The Souls of White Folk," he observes a phenomenon. "Wave upon wave, each with increasing virulence, is dashing this new religion of whiteness on the shores of our time."[13] By "new religion of whiteness," Du Bois is referring to the evolving tendency of whites to collectively take on whiteness as a social identity. What made it a religion was not just this identification but the fact that those who identified as white also believed that the identification made them exclusively special. They were now "white and by that token, wonderful."[14]

This wonderfulness, they believed, also granted them certain entitlements, manifested in imperialistic projects, according to Du Bois. He refers to this as the "right to ownership of the earth, forever and ever, Amen!"[15] Ownership was not only of the land and sea. Whiteness made white people feel entitled to the bodies that dwelt there. To remember whiteness and keep it holy, then, is a racial rule that tells us that we should recognize and remember the glory in and of whiteness—for this glory is a trait that is exclusive to whiteness and lacking in other people.

When Scottish philosopher David Hume wrote, "I am apt to suspect the negroes, and in general all the other species of men (for there are four or five different kinds) to be naturally inferior to the whites. There never was a civilized nation of any other complexion than white, nor even any individual eminent either in action or speculation. No ingenious manufactures amongst them, no arts, no sciences," he was endorsing the cognitive aspect of racial rule #1.[16] When US representative Steve King of Iowa asked, at the 2016 Republican National Convention, for us "to go back through history and figure out where are these contributions that have been made by these other categories of people you are talking about. Where did any other subgroup of people contribute more to civilization [than Europeans]?" he was endorsing the cognitive aspect of racial rule #1.[17] Fast-forward to 2019. When at a gathering with supporters in Sioux City, Iowa, King said that Western civilization "is a superior civilization. It exists everywhere where Judeo-Christianity laid the footprint for civilization,"[18] once again, he was endorsing racial rule #1. While these examples are explicit, we too can enforce this racial rule, at least implicitly, when we only read or teach white intellectuals or only hire white employees.

Hume, Steve King, and others did not wake up one random day and create racial rule #1. They learned it. And we all learn this racial rule—for as Du Bois witnessed in the beginning of the twentieth century and what is also currently the case in the West particularly, we are implicitly and explicitly taught that every great man, thought, or deed is connected to whiteness. The racial rule says that we ought to think this is true. This is a cognitive rule.

How does Lordean rage break the cognitive aspect of this racial rule? Remember that Lordean rage is directed at racists, racism, and the assumptions that undergird it. The assumption behind racism in the United States is white supremacy. In white supremacy, whiteness is superior and Blackness, Nativeness, Brownness, and so on, are inferior; American history is the history of this order being imposed, often violently and cruelly. But Lordean rage arises as a protest to this claim. It denies its truth and protests its assumptions.

When a person has Lordean rage, his anger arises not only because he detects that *something* is wrong. That description is too narrow and, in part, abstract. Rather, he detects that *particular claims* are wrong. One of those claims is that whiteness is superior. Since the racial rule says that we should accept the glory of whiteness (i.e., white supremacy), the very act of responding with Lordean rage breaks that racial rule. White supremacy is meant to be the status quo, the background to everyday life. It aims at determining whose life is valuable, whose rights should be respected, who should represent humanity, and who should be dominated. Responding to white supremacy with rage not only proclaims that supremacist thinking is incorrect, but it refuses to accept it, thus breaking the cognitive aspect of the racial rule in the process.

There are other implications of racial rule #1. It also says that we should not challenge but rather endorse white entitlement to land and peoples since they are within whiteness's right to possess. We learn this rule, which also is the theme of US history, from the moment Europeans crossed the ocean and landed on Indigenous peoples' land. As part of the status quo, we come to expect whiteness as the default, and we are often instructed to act in ways that help maintain white entitlement.

We learn to treat preferentially those racialized as white, pushing down all others in order to elevate whites. We are often rewarded as a result. We come to think that whiteness not only entitles people to dominance over land and nonwhite people but also possession of certain jobs, fame, wealth, school admissions, and neighborhoods. We act accordingly by either being silent in the face of such entitlement or ensuring it—often at the denial of opportunity or mistreatment of racialized others. This is the behavioral aspect of racial rule #1.

How does Lordean rage break this behavioral aspect of the racial rule? Remember the perspective that informs Lordean rage: "We are not free until we all are free." This perspective not only informs the rage but also motivates action. A person with Lordean rage is not motivated to engage in actions in which justice, rights, and opportunities are exclusive to a particular group. She aims to gain access for all. A person who responds to racial rule #1 with rage breaks the behavioral aspect of racial rule #1 by refusing to work to ensure that one group (whites) dominates at the expense of others.

Feeling rules are also present in racial rule #1. In the religion of whiteness, those who are not born white are instructed, according to Du Bois, "not to weep or rage but to be brave—for if they work hard enough on earth, they may return to it as white."[19] The rule prescribes for the racially oppressed courage over resentment, fearlessness over sadness. When racial minorities, in particular, challenge white entitlement and respond to imperialistic projects with anger instead of appreciation, they are punished. To summarize Du Bois, they are considered a threat and are viewed by those in power as ungrateful—proving to whites that racist claims are indeed tenable.[20] This shows the affective aspect of racial rule #1.

But Lordean rage breaks the affective aspect of this racial rule by resisting the recommendation not to express or even feel rage. It resists the recommendation by its mere presence as well as its continuation. The way you are supposed to feel, as a Black person, is not angry but brave and hopeful—hopeful that you, as a Black person, will one day be counted among the entitled (i.e., white) in *another lifetime*. Not today, but someday. And that's supposed to be enough to keep you happy enough to keep going. By refusing this prescription, by asking for more—for justice today, not tomorrow—Lordean rage defies the racial rules that are meant to keep people from overturning racial domination by whites.

The racial status quo not only depends on Black people hoping for racial justice someday (but not today) but also on making them hope that if they can't be treated as a full person, despite being Black, at least they can be treated as if they are white-adjacent: *almost* human. If Black people earn the right to be treated as white-adjacent, they can at least reap some benefits of white supremacy. How can a Black person achieve this almost-privileged status? Perhaps through political party affiliation, economic status, or educational achievement. These pathetically deficient reasons for hope—these options meant to inspire optimism that, if you scrutinize them, break your heart—are all part of the feeling rules that Lordean rage rejects. Lordean rage says to throw out your hope for *eventual* justice; throw out your striving to be treated *almost* as well as if you were white. Embrace your anger. Ask for more *now*.

There is yet another affective aspect. Part of remembering whiteness and keeping it holy is recognizing that when whiteness fails to act holy—whether through racial violence or other racial wrongdoings—it is met with forgiveness, not judgment or punishment. (In other words, part of the privilege of whiteness is getting the benefit of the doubt when you do wrong.) This response is not due to moral reasons. It is based on race. The frequency with which public forgiveness requests are made to Black victims of white violence and mistreatment, as well as the short time between the wrongdoing and the inquiry, provide some evidence of this.

Consider the recent high-profile cases of police violence and private acts of racism against Blacks in the United States. When officers shot and killed Philando Castile and Samuel DuBose, reporters asked their families quite quickly after the deaths if they would forgive the shooters. Castile's and DuBose's bodies had yet to be buried before the requests were made. A reporter asked Esaw Garner if she accepted the apology of the NYPD officer who put her husband—Eric Garner—in a chokehold in 2014 that many believed killed him. The reporter asked the question immediately after the courts decided not to indict the officers. In 2020, after a white woman, Amy Cooper, in a 911 call falsely accused Black birdwatcher Christian Cooper of threatening her, she apologized a few days later. Immediately afterward, reporters asked him if he would accept her apology. He replied, "If it's genuine and if she plans on keeping her dog on a leash in the Ramble going forward, then we have no issues with each other." In other work, I refer to this phenomenon of immediately asking and expecting Black forgiveness (or accepting apologies) in the aftermath of white violence and mistreatment as the *hurry and bury ritual*. The affective norm of racial rule #1 is to forgive whites (which is to say to forswear anger, according to the influential view of forgiveness) and expect that others will forgive them, because they are white.

One way of breaking this affective aspect of the rule is to refuse to give up one's rage by not forgiving, or at least not doing it immediately. Esaw Garner responded to the reporter's inquiry with, "Hell no! The time for remorse would have been when my husband was yelling to breathe." When two white men murdered twenty-five-year-old Ahmaud Arbery in Georgia for apparently jogging while Black in early 2020, some took notice of his mother's response. Instead of offering forgiveness, Wanda Cooper-Jones expressed her wish that the law enact retribution on his killers. When explaining the source of their anger, Marcus Arbery Sr. replied, "My son was lynched!" Rightfully, forgiveness was not the response that they had in that moment of pain and shock.

I am not claiming that there are never reasons for Blacks to forgive whites. I am only pointing to the ways in which social practices of forgiveness (which includes forgiveness requests) are racialized. What wrongs are forgiven (racial wrongs), whom we expect to forgive (Blacks), and the social space in which forgiveness requests are often made (a public space of asymmetrical power relations) show the multiple connections between race and practices of forgiveness.[21] More importantly, I am claiming that when nonwhites refuse to give up their anger out of a rejection of what I have described as "white holiness," they break the affective component of racial rule #1.

This combination of cognitive, behavioral, and feeling rules is constitutive of rule #1. Together these components ensure that racial rule #1 is followed. Someone responding to racism with Lordean rage is breaking these rules. But how is this affective transgression through Lordean rage important for the anti-racist struggle? White supremacy depends on racial rule #1 as well as its cognitive, behavioral, and affective aspects. A person who responds to this racial rule through Lordean rage rejects white supremacists' claims and logics, defying the constraints that are supposed to limit her emotions and behavior. And when those constraints are based on race, the act of resisting them is a powerful act of resisting racism and racial injustice. Thus, the affective transgression of having and valorizing Lordean rage is important for anti-racist struggle.

Rule #2: Thou Shall Not Have a Right to White Male Anger

In a Root.com video series, author Damon Young—in asking the question "Why are white men so angry?"—begins with a sense of bewilderment. After all, as he points out, white men run Fortune 500 companies and are most of the elected officials and police officers in the United States. When white men look at any denomination of US paper currency, they see their faces on it. "America is basically Wakanda for white men," he says, highlighting their total dominance, but "despite all of this they are angry." White male anger is puzzling for Young because he can't understand what they could possibly have to be angry about: they have the most power, wealth, and control of any demographic, and they often exert their power over others, to the disadvantage of every other group.

Young has a point. Many of us, especially those in groups that lack advantages because of dominance exerted by white men— sometimes occupying intersectional identities that make us doubly or triply disadvantaged, in comparison to white men—share in Young's bewilderment. It is hard not to wonder how members of the dominant class think they have moral reasons to be angry. One could argue that Young's assessment is reductive since not *all* white men run companies or govern cities, and some men have less privilege than we tend to assume when we think of white men as a broad category. (They too can have identities and be in groups that make them suffer hardships—for example, if they are gay, disabled, or socioeconomically disadvantaged.) But I see another issue that's worth our inquiry. Young's comments imply that reasons for anger are only rooted in resources, opportunity, and the lack thereof. For him, if white men do not lack these things, then they lack moral reasons to be angry. But I think more is going on.

While examining whether people have reasons to be angry—reasons related to material access—seems like a good test to hold people to when examining their rage, if we only focus on these reasons we fail to understand the nature of racialized emotions and the connection between value, respect, and anger. Making sense of both can help explain what is happening in the case Young is interested in and racial rule #2.

Once again, feminist philosophers provide some helpful framing here. In particular, we should start with the way they have theorized gendered emotions. Some feminist philosophers have claimed that different norms govern behavior and emotions for different socially positioned people.[22] The norms are there so that each member can fulfill their expected social role. This social role accords them different duties, as well as differing amounts of power. As it pertains to gender, women and men are expected to conform to the norms that govern their respective gendered roles in society. The roles are in part determined by cultural ideas as well as biological and psychological stereotypes. The particular traits that assist people with fulfilling their roles are termed "masculine" and "feminine." When men display so-called masculine traits, the traits are considered virtues. When men display feminine traits, those traits are considered vices. Men are traditionally expected to fulfill a military and protective role, so masculine traits would include strength and aggressiveness. Emotions that express these masculine traits, such as anger, are often expected of men. (In this way, emotions are also gendered.) And these emotions are viewed as virtues as a result. Given men's power in society and their assumed rationality, their anger is likely to be given uptake by others.

Women, on the other hand, are traditionally expected to take care of the family, so feminine traits include gentleness and humility since they help women fulfill their social role. Emotions that express these feminine traits, such as compassion, are expected of women. As a result, it is considered a virtue for women to behave compassionately. Anger, on the other hand, is a masculine trait and is considered a vice for women. Given women's lack of power in society and their perceived irrationality, it is not surprising that when they express their anger, they are likely to be dismissed as bitter. They are also likely to be dismissed as hysterical since anger felt or expressed by women is by definition not fitting—just because of who they are.

But just as there are gendered roles and emotions, in my view there are also racialized roles and emotions. Moreover, certain norms also govern these roles—norms informed by racial ideas as well as biological and psychological stereotypes of racial groups. Different racial groups also have different duties and degrees of power. We might describe racial roles, preliminarily, as belonging to one or the other of two simple categories: control (for whites) and submission (for racial others). Given the racial role of control, traits such as aggressiveness and intelligence are considered a virtue in whites, for they help whites fulfill their role. When displayed in Blacks, however, these traits will likely be judged as vices.[23] Emotions like anger are expected of whites for they express their social power and rationality; also—as we will see—anger allows them to enforce white supremacy. Anger for Blacks, on the other hand, is considered a vice because it does not help them fulfill their submissive role. Anger in Blacks, as well as in other racial groups, is out of place, unfitting, and dangerous.[24]

Given the above analysis, how then might we begin to make sense of white anger and racial rule #2? The answer is painfully simple. Anger is what whites have a right to feel since it helps them fulfill their racial role. It is their right as well as their duty. While nonwhites have a right to some emotions, they do not have a right to anger because of their inferior social role.

Seeing the connection between anger, value, and respect also helps us understand Young's case as well as racial rule #2: that if you are not white, you do not have a right to white male anger. Philosophers since Aristotle have made claims about the connection between anger and respect. A person who is not angry at a moral violation done against himself is, according to Aristotle, a fool and not self-respecting.[25] Contemporary philosophers have argued that a moral wrongdoing promotes the message, "You do not matter."

Anger in response to wrongdoing says, "I do not endorse that message."[26] A person who submits to being wronged and does not protest against it is considered a person lacking in self-respect, but this does not imply that the protest must take on an angry form.

Given this connection, one can understand the self-respect Frederick Douglass felt after his angry protest against the slave breaker Covey. When Covey attempted to beat Douglass in order to make him more submissive, Douglass protested by physically resisting Covey's attempts. Recalling the incident later in his autobiographies, Douglass described it as a "turning point in my career as a slave. It rekindled the few expiring embers of freedom, and revived within me a sense of my own manhood. It recalled the departed self-confidence."[27] By pushing back on his mistreatment, he was saying he did not endorse the disrespect that Covey showed him. Douglass, as an abolitionist, would continue to express anger at slavery in his speeches and journalism. In doing so, he transgressed the racial rules by being both Black and angry—thus posing a threat to the natural order by which anger was the sole domain of powerful whites, like Covey. Not surprisingly, then, when nineteenth-century feminist Elizabeth Cady Stanton recalled first hearing Douglass, she noted that "he stood there like an African prince, majestic in his wrath, as with wit, satire, and indignation he graphically described the bitterness of slavery and the humiliation of subjection."[28]

In a context of racial domination, it will be assumed that only those in power have enough value to warrant respect. It logically follows that only they get to feel and express anger when that respect is violated. People who are part of the racially dominated group would not have such value, and therefore would have no claims to respect and thus no right to anger. Part of nonwhites' racial subordination then would be to deny them such respect and to teach them to lack it within themselves. So, while the dominant racial group has a right to be angry, others, like Douglass and Esaw Garner, have no such right.

In addition, it can be argued that "righteous" white anger operates as a law enforcement wing of white supremacy.[29] By *righteous white anger* (*RWA*), I am referring to the anger that whites think they are entitled to because they are white. The perceived wrongdoers whom RWA responds to are often nonwhites—think of Amy Cooper's anger at Christian Cooper (no relation) in Central Park. The wrongdoings that RWA responds to are social role violations and what I call *acts of existence*. Contrasted with acts of resistance, which often require *action*, acts of existence simply require *being*. Whites can harass others not because they are *doing* anything wrong but because they are simply living, laughing, birdwatching, running, or walking while Black, Mexican, trans, or Arab.[30] The very act of being can provide reason for the harassment. RWA enforces and polices racial rules by responding to threats against (white) law and order. When righteous white anger is on display, its aim is to uphold and patrol white norms pertaining to value and respect.

RWA was on display at the 2017 white nationalist march in Charlottesville, Virginia. One way we can interpret the marchers' angry chant ("You will not replace us!") is as an expression of whites' dominant place within a racial hierarchy and their commitment to protecting their rank—and the privileges and entitlements that come along with it. RWA was also on display at the Capitol Hill insurrection to overturn the US elections in 2021.

But we ought not think that only white nationalists or insurrectionists express RWA. White citizens engaging in ordinary life can also express it. For example, in 2018, witnesses filmed two women (who became known online as "Permit Patty" and "Barbeque Becky") using their righteous white anger (combined with police threats and even tears) to police Black movement and protect white space. In the case of Permit Patty, all it took to inspire her anger was a Black girl selling water outside of a New York office building. In the case of Barbeque Becky, the so-called offense that set off her anger was the sight of Black adults legally barbequing in an Oakland public park. Recall the Central Park case, when Christian Cooper was doing nothing more than politely reminding the white woman of the park rules regarding dogs. In response, she called the cops to tell them that a Black man was threatening her and her dog. The so-called offense I suppose that set off her anger was that a Black person was reminding her of rule-breaking. But based on the logic of RWA, her job is to police him, not the other way around. Obviously, in none of these instances were actual laws being broken, and in none of these cases were these activities that would have caused anyone—not even busybodies like Patty and Becky—any alarm if whites had performed them. These are examples of what has come to be known as manifestations of "Karen" at work—a trope that describes white women who police others (and call the police on them) over minor inconveniences. Karens also weaponize their white womanhood in ways that are dangerous for nonwhites. These cases show the reality of RWA in everyday life and how it is often used to police racial minorities' actions, being, and the public space they inhabit. Even though racial rule #2 refers to the anger of white men, this anger can be shared with white women when it is in the service of white supremacy.

Not only is it possible for those with racial power to feel that only they have a right to be angry, but they may also think that nonwhites, given their perceived low status, will have no real reasons to be angry. How is this possible? Our perception of a racial group and the claims they are allowed to lay hold to will determine what emotions they have a right to. If a group holds no real power or is judged to have no true value, then when members of that group are mistreated, outsiders may be less likely to think that they have been insulted. And the group would also seem to have no right to be angry as a result.

This analysis becomes a lot easier to grasp when we look at some examples and the way they exemplify racial rule #2 and how it is enforced. Consider three Black women whose anger has garnered public attention and criticism: Serena Williams, Sandra Bland, and Anita Hill.

Some might think that US tennis player Serena Williams has experienced unfair calls and racial mistreatment from referees and fellow players throughout her career. We can cite white Danish player Caroline Wozniacki imitating Serena's Black body by stuffing towels in her top and bottom in an exhibition game; umpires making notable bad calls (recall Mariana Alves at the 2004 US Open, who made a number of unfair judgments against Serena) and officials punishing her for her angry response; and a sportswriter accusing her of lacking integrity and holding a grudge for boycotting the Indian Wells Masters tennis tournament, a place where people had hurled racial slurs at Serena and Venus Williams in the past. Describing Serena's anger and people's reaction to it in *Citizen*, poet Claudia Rankine writes,

> Because her body, trapped in a racial imaginary, trapped in disbelief— code for being black in America—is being governed not by the tennis match she is participating in but by a collapsed relationship that had promised to play by the rules. Perhaps this is how racism feels no matter the context—randomly the rules everyone else gets to play by no longer apply to you, and to call this out . . . is to be called insane, crass, crazy, and bad sportsmanship.[31]

We can see a connection between value, respect, and anger happening here. If others view Serena as having no inherent value outside of the financial value she provides to the sport, then she will have no claims to respect and thus no reason to be angry. Even if she does experience mistreatment, it will be hard for others (especially the predominantly white viewership of professional tennis) to see it as such. Perhaps this explains the public outcry about her outrage and a discounting of her rage as irrational, aggressive, crazy, and unsportsmanlike—all of which have been reflected in media coverage of her over the years. While white male tennis stars like Novak Djokovic can express anger on the court, Serena does not have this right.

Or take the example of someone much less famous. Sandra Bland was a Black woman who was found dead in her jail cell days after being pulled over by a police officer in Texas in 2015 for failing to signal. During the recorded traffic stop, we can see her righteous indignation (as well as her fear) in her responses at being asked to put out her cigarette, and then step out of her car for a refusal to do so, and at being physically mishandled by the officer. The officer then arrested Bland. (Of course for him, Bland was not indignant but rather aggravated and dangerous.)[32] If we consider her case from the perspective of a white-supremacist patriarchy, she would be perceived to have no inherent value, and therefore her claims of being disrespected by the officer would sound untenable. As a Black woman, by definition she would not be worthy of respect; she wouldn't have the respect in the first place, so the police could not take it away by disrespecting her. And if she is not being disrespected, her indignation would be hard to understand by those who watch the video encounter. Perhaps this explains why suggestions of what she should have done (followed police instructions) rang louder than the public outcry of how she was handled. Three days after her arrest, Bland hung herself in her jail cell.

Law professor Anita Hill is most known for her 1991 testimony to members of the US Senate about sexual harassment by then–Supreme Court nominee Clarence Thomas—claims that stirred up multiple divisions but also introduced the concept of sexual harassment into the public imaginary. In Hill's comments about the 2018 hearings involving Supreme Court nominee Brett Kavanaugh and Dr. Christine Blasey Ford, Hill confirms the affective gendered asymmetry that is very much like feeling rules and gendered emotion norms. "[Kavanaugh] was able to express a real anger, an aggression, as well as a lot of emotion. . . . No female Supreme Court candidate," she said, "would ever have the license to express [herself] in that way."[33] Truth is, not only did there exist a gender asymmetry in relationship to emotions, but both Hill's and Ford's case point out a racial one as well.

Hill's anger was heavily criticized because it was racialized at the time of her testimony. Even while remaining calm, she, unlike Ford, was painted as angry. She was also perceived as "acting uppity" for thinking "her rights had been denied."[34] Here we see the logic once more. As a Black woman, Hill had no perceived value. Her value was a faux value, as the trivializing term "uppity" (itself a racialized term) implies. She at least had no value that a Black man and the white Senate committee members were under any obligation to respect. If she had no perceived value, we can see how her claims to respect in the workplace were judged to be unwarranted, and thus her anger was perceived not only as exaggerated but inapt.

While we can learn a lot from the example of these three women, we need to look at a final example in order to further grasp the absurdity of rejections to claims of anger in response to racial mistreatment.

In 2014, white police officer Daren Wilson fatally shot Black teenager Michael Brown. Wilson told Brown to get out of the street, and Brown responded with what Wilson interpreted as disrespect. Given this disrespect (and racial rules #1 and #2), Officer Wilson had a right to respond to the insult. Brown, unfortunately, was thought to have no such right. We can see this in Wilson's description of what happened after he shot Brown.

> He looked up at me and had the most intense aggressive face. The only way I can describe it, it looks like a demon, that's how angry he looked.... He was almost bulking up to run through the shots, like it was making him mad that I'm shooting him.

Wilson is surprised that Brown showed anger at being shot—as if Brown had no rational reason to be angry that he was being shot, as any human being would be. Even while dying, Brown had no claim to insult and respect and thus no claim to anger. In a white-supremacist, male-dominated society, this is how things ought to be. Blacks will have no claims to respect and thus anger—and they are likely to be punished for assuming that they do.

In a capitalist, white-supremacist society, *poor* Black people in particular would have no right to be respected or angry. Michael Brown was not a Black celebrity, member of the elite, or college educated. He was a resident of a Black, rural, working-class community. Perhaps this also matters to how he was viewed and treated. Brown's failure to do anything on the capital market could have figured into his Black body being perceived as lacking value and respect, and thus lacking reasons to be angry even while being shot.[35] Let's return to Du Bois's "The Souls of White Folk":

> So long, then, as humble black folk, voluble with thanks, receive barrels of old clothes from lordly and generous whites, there is much mental

peace and moral satisfaction. But when the black man begins to dispute the white man's title to certain alleged bequests of the Fathers in wage and position, authority and training; and when his attitude toward charity is sullen anger rather than humble jollity; when he insists on his human right to swagger and swear and waste, then the spell is suddenly broken and the philanthropist is ready to believe that Negroes are impudent, that the South is right.[36]

Brown is denied a right to anger even in the midst of fatal assault. Poor Blacks like Brown—as Du Bois pointed out over one hundred years ago, and as clearly remains true—are expected to be grateful for police intervention in what some might describe as their violent, dysfunctional communities. Poor Blacks are expected to respond to the police, who are actors of the state, with gratitude, not anger. An angry response expresses ungratefulness, not respect. It is inapt in both cases, one might think, thereby making it surprising that poor Blacks' anger exists in the first place.

Contrast these examples with elite white men. When Dr. Ford accused Brett Kavanaugh of sexual assault, he wasn't merely allowed to express anger—it was expected that he would do so. On some accounts, he had to because the accusations were taking away from him the respect to which he felt he, as a white man, was entitled.[37] Here we see the connection between respect and entitlement. I can be angry at being disrespected, but what I perceive as disrespect depends on the level and kind of respect to which I believe I am entitled. So, while we are likely to see high degrees of anger among people who face significant levels of harm and disrespect, we are also likely to find high degrees of anger among people with significant levels of entitlement.

It stands to reason that this will not only apply to those who believe they themselves are so entitled but also to those who believe that others are so entitled. They are likely to feel high degrees of anger on behalf of those they believe have significant levels of entitlement. Perhaps this explains why Kavanaugh was able to galvanize a generation of older white women angry on behalf of their sons whom they saw as potential victims of women's accusations.[38]

These examples not only show the relationship between value, respect, and anger, but they also reveal the cognitive, behavioral, and affective aspects of racial rule #2. The cognitive rule says that we should accept the perceived lack of value of certain lives. In a capitalist, white-supremacist, male-dominated society, some lives are valuable, other lives are not. Those lives that are valuable are typically white, wealthy, able-bodied, and cis-male. Lives that hold less value usually have the opposite identities to those that are valued: Black, Brown, woman, poor, disabled, trans, and so on. But if anger is a way of valuing, as I argue in Chapter 2, and if anger is a way to respond to such value, then when a person has Lordean rage in response to racism, one is breaking this racial rule. Through rage, a person is rejecting claims that only some lives are valuable—and rage does this by proclaiming that all lives are valuable.

Even when a person has Lordean rage but is part of the racially dominant group, the rule remains. These people too are instructed not to waste their anger on a group that, in the dominant view, has no claims to respect. While white people with Lordean rage may be viewed as race traitors, they are, particularly in this case, best described as *rage renegades*—using rage that is supposed to be reserved to defend respect that's exclusive to whites in the service of all lives that suffer insults and disrespect. (We discuss rage renegades more in Chapter 5.)

Racial rule #2 also has a behavioral aspect. If a person does not have a right to white-male anger, then to ensure that the rule is followed, there must be consequences for not following it. The behavioral aspect of the rule is also an enforcement rule. It says: Don't demand respect if you are nonwhite, and act civilly and respectfully toward white people in the face of insult or you will be punished. Lordean rage resists these commands and challenges racial mistreatment. By doing so, it breaks the rule about who gets to be respected, while accepting that there may be consequences for doing so. Some people, in breaking this rule and demanding respect either for themselves or others, can pay for their transgression with their very lives. But this is not the only punishment people experience. Some people break this rule at the risk of confirming negative stereotypes (e.g., all Black women are angry or all Latinas are sassy), being rejected by powerful networks, or being labeled as the threatening minority. Those with Lordean rage often take the risks of having anger without knowing which punishment, if any, will come their way.

The affective dimension of racial rule #2 says that given the cognitive and behavioral dimensions, anger at racism should never be experienced, and if it is, it should be suppressed. Since anger is only the right of whites and should only be in response to their mistreatment, not just anyone has a right to it. The affective aspect—similar to racial rule #1—commands that certain people forswear or suppress their anger, perhaps even replace it with something else.

But since Lordean rage has a specific target (racism) and aim (change), it cannot be so easily replaced. It exists to do something, not to merely disappear. And Lordean rage breaks this affective aspect of the rule by experiencing and expressing itself. As I discuss in Chapter 6, expression comes in different degrees and types. But we need for our purposes here to keep in mind one important detail about expression.

Whether I have a small or large audience, or whether I express anger to myself, acknowledging that Lordean rage exists, even privately, will still break this aspect of the rule. While anger itself, as well as its public acknowledgment, can be communicative, a person does not require a large audience to make claims about their value. Even plantation slaves who did not take the risk that Frederick Douglass did to publicly announce themselves as self-respecting through anger could still break this racial rule if they only had an audience of one—themselves. If domination also includes the psychological sphere, resisting it in one's own mind is just as much a radical act as resisting in the face of the oppressor or in front of a crowd.

When we take this broad view of anger and acknowledge that sometimes being inwardly angry is resistance in itself, we have to look at President Barack Obama's perceived lack of anger in a different light. In public discourse during his presidency, much was made of the fact that he was never angry. Given the trope of the angry Black man, the fact that he was the first Black person to hold the country's highest office and faced a certain level of scrutiny that only the president gets, we can see why Obama was cautious with expressing anger. Despite media attacks, claims that he was not American or Christian, racist cartoons of him and his family, and verbal disrespect from politicians (recall Representative Joe Wilson who yelled, "You lie!" at Obama during a 2009 joint Congress address), Obama never *publicly* expressed anger. But some members of the Black community did not doubt that anger was there. They knew all too well that even for a Black president, keeping one's anger below the radar in a society where racial domination commands such rules is important. But it was definitely there, even for someone as "cool" as Obama.

The Comedy Central sketch show *Key and Peele* created the character Luther, Obama's anger translator, as a satirical way to give (a hypothetical) voice to what they thought was Obama's unexpressed "public" anger. The sketch clearly resonated with Obama himself, since he asked Luther to make an appearance with him at the 2015 White House Correspondents Dinner. At the dinner, standing beside Obama himself, Luther translates President Obama's live speech in an angry, dramatic, yet comedic fashion. But then Obama begins to express his own anger as he explains what he takes to be politicians' irresponsible response to climate change. Luther is taken aback by this and tries to calm Obama down. The audience laughs. This bit could be read as endorsing the interpretation that the comic skit originally meant to convey: Obama did experience and express anger, and he had to carefully monitor himself lest it come out in public. However, Obama didn't need to advertise his anger in order to break racial rules. Simply by experiencing it, he broke racial rules.[39] So can you.

* * *

Experiencing Lordean rage is an act of resistance. Before or after movements are started, massive protests occur, negotiations are had, or policies adopted, those with Lordean rage break racial rules. This is itself part of revolutionary struggle. If this is the case, then the features of resistance figures we encountered at the beginning of this chapter are not necessary. We need not do something particular with our rage to be a resistance figure. A person can be a resistance figure by breaking racial rules. This does not deny the importance of using anger to tackle structures of power through massive protests. But large-scale organizing is not the only way to resist racial domination. For this reason, while we tend to only praise charismatic leaders and revolutionary justice figures for their political aims and courage to speak truth to power, Lordean rage teaches us that hidden resistance figures dwell among us—people who break racial rules through their anger as a way to disrupt and resist racial domination.

When we start to recognize Lordean rage in all its magnificent forms, we begin to see what is all too often invisible or overlooked: the daily contribution of those whose racial rule-breaking through anti-racist anger reveals racial logics, blocks white supremacist plans, resists claims of superiority, grants respect to all persons, affirms the value of racialized groups, and disrupts racial domination by any means necessary.

5

Rage Renegades

A Special Message to "Allies"

In response to the police killings in 2020 of George Floyd in Minneapolis, Minnesota; Breonna Taylor in Louisville, Kentucky; and the deaths of other Black people at the hands of police, Americans and those in solidarity with them around the world marched to protest racism, racial inequality, and police brutality. Reportedly, seventy protests per week occurred in US cities during the spring and summer of that year. The city receiving the majority of media attention was Portland, Oregon. At the time of this writing, Portland activists have been protesting for over 120 days. While some events were violent, most of them were not. (Nevertheless, conservative media and politicians referred to demonstrations there as "rioting" and "looting," hoping to stir up fear that would drive voters to reelect Trump, the self-appointed law-and-order candidate.) But it's not just the duration or politicization of the protests that makes Portland stand out in my mind. It's that the protests were happening in one of the whitest cities in America.[1] What's more, the protests had been overwhelmingly attended by whites.[2] This shows that it wasn't just racial minorities who were angry at racism. Whites were too.

Nor was it just young people protesting. Middle-aged white women (known as Portland's Wall of Moms) joined the protests, followed by the Wall of Dads and the Wall of Veterans—groups formed to protect front-line demonstrators from police. With fists raised, hands up, and clutched cardboard signs conveying messages like "White Silence = Violence," "Use your white privilege to end white privilege," and "This is a revolt against racism," many protestors expressed their solidarity with Blacks and their anger at racism. Some were arrested for their defiance—even grabbed by unidentified federal agents and placed in unmarked vans. Others like former navy officer Christopher J. David were tear-gassed and beaten with batons. After the video of the incident went viral, the fifty-three-year-old responded in an interview like a true white ally. "If I had been a Black veteran that had gotten beaten down, do you think I would have gotten as much attention as I did?" he asked the journalist rhetorically. To decenter himself and his whiteness he added, "It isn't about me getting beat up. It's about focusing back on the original intention of all of these protests, which is Black Lives Matter."[3]

* * *

Lordean rage is not just anger that racially marginalized people have in response to injustice. We would hope that people in solidarity with the oppressed—allies—will also have this anti-racist anger, particularly if they value all members of a society, judge that racial injustice is wrong, do not consider themselves free until all people are free, and aim to resist racist systems. These are the rage renegades whom we encountered earlier. They are rage renegades because although their privilege and place in a white-supremacist society is meant to guarantee that they will be complicit with or engage in racism as a way to maintain racial domination, they instead show outrage at this society. In doing so, they rebel against a racist system that was designed to benefit them.

Although allyship can be helpful to people and movements, allies must not behave in ways that maintain the very systems of oppression they are aiming to challenge and resist. We have already seen what those with Lordean rage can do with their rage in the anti-racist struggle: value, produce, and resist. But an ally with Lordean rage can also do negative things, and we need to be mindful of them. Renegade raging can go wrong. Starting out, it's important to note that simply having right intentions isn't a get-out-of-jail-free card. As philosopher Veronica Ivy (formerly Rachel McKinnon) has noted, "Coming to understand how to properly engage in an anti-racist project . . . is understanding . . . it's going to be a lot of work. . . . It's more work when you don't have the identity."[4]

If you have been tracking my taxonomy of rage carefully, you may be wondering, why a chapter on allyship and Lordean rage? It may sound strange to hear that my criticism will be directed toward those with Lordean rage instead of narcissistic rage—for it would be easy to think that allies who behave badly have transitioned from Lordean rage to the narcissistic kind. But remember, Lordean rage is not by definition virtuous. It too can go wrong, and so it can sometimes go wrong when it comes to allyship.[5]

By addressing this chapter to allies, I'm not implying that the racially oppressed are immune from any kind of wrongdoing when they have Lordean rage. Anyone can do wrong. But focusing on allies here provides a helpful window into the unique harms that rage renegades can potentially inflict. Likewise, my intention is not to focus on allies in order to call out white people or other racial groups. People go wrong as allies because they are human, not because they are one race or another. Nor is this about making people—making you—feel guilty. By taking a look at the challenges allies face, and the way their rage can go wrong, I hope to help allies guard against using their Lordean rage in ways that reify the very racist system to which the anger is responding.

All sorts of controversy exist when it comes to allies. Even the term "ally" is not without controversy. One common position is that we should abandon it entirely. Writer Ta-Nehisi Coates thinks we should do so because the term implies that racial justice is a fight for the marginalized alone. For Coates, we need to understand that when we join others in combating injustice, we "are not helping someone in a particular struggle; the fight is [ours]."[6] Veronica Ivy thinks the term "ally" focuses too much on who a person takes themselves to be rather than engaging in action to end oppression. Therefore, some have opted for the terms "co-conspirators," "co-agitators," "active bystanders," and "collaborators" to counter these worries.[7]

The *actions* of allies are also controversial. Grassroots activists and writers have illustrated the myriad ways in which allies can marginalize people of color—and they have shown us in the form of dos and don'ts, and critical analyses. Allies must be careful not to take breaks from being allies (the people whose allies they are don't get to take such breaks) or to monopolize the emotional energy of oppressed groups.[8] Allies must speak up, not over others, and they need to apologize when they make mistakes, as activist and comedian Franchesca Ramsey has said.[9] Ivy describes how allies can behave badly epistemically, that is, within the domain of knowledge. For example, allies may gaslight others and rely on their own experiences to counter people's testimonies of injustice.[10] Psychologists Lauren Mizock and Konjit Page explain that allies can reify social constructs and hierarchies, as well as reinforce hero-victim narratives.[11] And author Mychal Denzel Smith describes how allies use their ally identity in ways that "become self-congratulatory, centers their experience at the expense of the marginalized, and . . . reinforces oppressive behaviors."[12]

While Christopher J. David, the white Portland protester noted earlier, serves as an ally exemplar, Portland's Wall of Moms' (early) actions hit at these thinkers' concerns. Some local organizations accused them of anti-Blackness for excluding Black moms, failing to protect Black protestors, failing to consult Black leadership, and co-opting BLM for their own purposes.[13] They were allies behaving badly. Around the same time in Portland, an anonymous non-Black woman of color, dubbed "Naked Athena" on the internet, decided to use her body as a shield between demonstrators and federal agents in a different way than the wall groups. Describing her decision as the result of a fury that arose in her, she stood nude in front of agents— striking yoga poses while standing, spreading her legs open while sitting. Although she had good intentions, for some it was a moment that upstaged the movement.[14]

As these examples and criticisms have pointed out, allyship—the label *and* its participants—is fraught. There are lots of ways of doing it wrong. For our purposes, though, we need to examine the unique ways in which allies with Lordean rage can behave badly, in order to get us closer to a full picture of Lordean rage's role in the fight against racism. So how can allies do horrible things specifically *with* their Lordean rage?

Same Feelings ≠ Same Experience

One way in which renegade raging can go wrong is when allies think that their feelings in response to racism are equal to, synonymous with, or comparable to the feelings and realities of the oppressed. They might think that because they share in Lordean rage, they also feel the same as the oppressed. We might hear an ally say, "We are both angry," and mean it in ways that ignore the nuances of racism and how racism affects people's lives differently.

However, the same feeling does not equate to the same experience. Although we might have similar emotional responses to a target, this does not mean that we feel its impact in the same way. Although rage may unify us in solidarity, it does not unify us in a metaphysical sense; it does not literally make us one. A rage renegade behaves badly by ignoring this important difference.

As we've seen, after the deaths of George Floyd and Breonna Taylor, many white people were stirred by racism in the United States—particularly by the police against Black people—like never before. And this was a great development; people of all races and ethnicities took to the streets, statues of Confederate officers came down, buildings were renamed, some police reforms were put in place, and in various ways, small steps were made to get us closer to racial equality. But in the midst of this, had a white protestor claimed to know how her Black fellow-protestor felt in this heated moment, she would have misstepped. Not having lived as a Black person in this country, not having been raised to carry herself differently in order to navigate hostile spaces, the white protestor, despite her best intentions, just couldn't have really known.

Why is it different to feel *solidarity with* someone than to actually feel the way they feel? It's not because rage renegades have a different kind of anger, such as empathetic rage—the rage a person feels by imagining himself in the shoes of Dalits in India (people formerly designated as "untouchable" based on the caste system), for example—as opposed to the Lordean rage that many marginalized people feel. This kind of rage, at least for David Hume, is only an impression of what the oppressed person actually feels. If the rage renegade was feeling this rage, then the mistake he would be making would be clear: there is no way his rage could be the same as that of the oppressed Dalits since what he is feeling is only an impression of what members of the Dalit community are experiencing. However, I do not think rage renegades believe they are experiencing empathetic rage. Outraged allies often report that they are experiencing anger at racism—anger that someone is being racially oppressed and anger that they, themselves, live in a racially oppressive system. This is not vicarious anger. What they claim to have is the very same rage that the oppressed feel. So they are not in error because they are mistaken about the nature of their rage. They are making a different kind of error.

An ally, in thinking that he feels as the oppressed also feels, not only commits a metaphysical mistake but a moral one. He minimizes people's experiences of injustice and reduces them to an emotion. Our emotional experiences are never quite identical. More importantly, feeling Lordean rage in response to injustice is not the same as feeling what the oppressed feels—it is not the same as feeling the emotions that arise due to and as a result of the rage, such as vulnerability, victimization, and pain. Just because a person is outraged does not mean that they now have the phenomenology or face the discomforting and disheartening reality of racially oppressed people.

Not only should a rage renegade not think that they feel the same as the marginalized, they also shouldn't think that their Lordean rage now makes them *know how it feels* to be marginalized. This is an epistemic mistake. An ally might think that because they have Lordean rage, they understand oppressed people's experiences and what they are feeling in response to them. They might say, "I totally understand! I'm angry too," when an Asian American shares her experiences of discrimination. They convey through their response that they understand (or "over-stand" in this case) what the woman feels in a way that is overly confident, not sympathetic. They are overconfident because they think there is a strong link between their rage, as an ally, and knowledge—knowledge that can only come from the firsthand experience of injustice.

Having said that, there is still a connection between knowledge and anger. As we saw earlier in Chapter 2, Lordean rage involves knowledge of racism. Also, feminists have argued, quite convincingly, that anger has epistemic advantages.[15] Anger can "enable us to perceive the world differently than we would from its portrayal in conventional descriptions . . . [and it] may provide the first indications that something is wrong with the way alleged facts have been constructed, with accepted understandings of how things are," according to Alison Jaggar.[16] However, having Lordean rage does not make anyone a know-it-all about oppression. If you think you already know something, you do not listen when someone explains it to you. If a person thinks she knows all about how another person truly feels because she too is angry about racism, she blocks herself from remaining curious, humble, and open to continually learning about the experiences of the marginalized and the reality of racism. We do not learn this by being angry. We learn it by listening to the experiences of others and giving up willful ignorance, to name just a couple of ways. These activities are what allies should be engaged in. Knowledge is not transferred through emotional experiences alone. We obtain it through hard, sympathetic, patient, and humble work. For this reason, we can understand the original criticisms of Portland's Wall of Moms. No matter what emotions they may have felt for Black lives and expressed at the system, their critics believed that their initial failure to listen to local Black leadership limited their allyship and caused harm.

Allowing Lordean rage to engender a false certainty prevents learning and awareness—both of which are needed in order to engage in anti-racist struggle. But ignorance and lack of awareness also prevent allies from seeing their unique position. Rage renegades should recognize where they stand in relation to the racially marginalized. No matter how much rage they may have, they are still more privileged and socially positioned in ways the racially marginalized are not. As a result, allies are in a position to harm and help in specific ways. In order to guard against harming and engage in helping instead, they must not forget where they stand. Having Lordean rage is a good thing. But when allies think their rage makes them know what it is like or how it feels to be oppressed by a racist society, it doesn't do anyone any good.

When White Anger Matters More

Another way in which rage renegades can behave badly is when they think that their anger matters more than the anger of the racially marginalized.

As we saw earlier, value, respect, and anger are connected.[17] If a person thinks that he has value, when he is mistreated he will feel he has been denied the respect that he deserves, and he will have a right to be angry in response. When we look at Western history, it is white men—not Indigenous peoples—who have been said to have legitimate claims to anger. While of course people of all races—including white people—can be denied respect and feel rage as a result, society has been structured in such a way that only whites were assumed to start out with legitimate respect, so that taking that respect away would be worthy of anger. As we know, nonwhites have frequently been disrespected—often because of who they are, racially. But because they didn't start out with the social perception of deserving respect, denying them respect would not be (for dominant whites) worthy of their anger. ("Why should a person get angry for denying them something they don't deserve?") As a result, the way we perceive anger is deeply racialized—it reads different depending on who has it.

Just as whites are seen as having more of a claim to anger than nonwhites, men are often seen as being more righteous in their anger than women. The 2018 Brett Kavanaugh and Dr. Christine Blasey Ford Senate hearings illustrate this. But at the end of the day, when it comes to rage, race matters. Many white women believe they have claims to anger. We can again recall Amy Cooper's rage in Central Park, when Christian Cooper simply asked her to leash her dog. Out of self-preservation, Christian Cooper stayed calm as he could be throughout the now-viral interaction. Amy Cooper felt no shame in raising her voice when she called the police—she assumed they would be on her side. She hadn't been conditioned to temper her emotions as Christian Cooper had, due to the privilege that is conferred on her due to her race. As Eduardo Bonilla-Silva's work shows us, this illustrates the racial asymmetry of feeling rules.[18] In a white-supremacist society, some people's emotions (and their claims to value and respect) will be accepted, while other people's emotions will not be—and this will be based on racial identity.

A 2019 *Saturday Night Live* skit titled "Impossible Hulk" illustrates quite brilliantly the value of the anger (and fear) of white women in comparison to Black men. In the skit, Black British actor Idris Elba plays Bruce Banner, a scientist who has an accident in his lab. As a result of the accident, Bruce transforms into an "emboldened white lady when he is provoked." There are different scenes in which he transforms. Each instance highlights the difference between how his anger is viewed as a Black man versus when he is a white woman.

While shopping in a clothing store, Bruce pays for a shirt he thinks is a certain price. When he realizes the price is different from advertised, he asks for a refund. However, the white cashier refuses to give him his money back. He protests and reports that he is about to get angry. The cashier then threatens to call security. Soon Bruce transforms into an emboldened white woman—what the internet would call a "Karen." As a white woman, he proclaims, "I want my money back right now!" He then proceeds to call the police with his cell phone. In response, the cashier tells him to take his money back and that it's fine to do so. This is a very different reaction than the one he received as a Black man. His anger is respected when he is a white woman but not when he is a Black man. It's a hilarious satirical sketch, but the point that underlies it is a very serious one, resulting from racism, injustice, and oppression: the respect that is given to his anger is connected to the perceived legitimacy of his claims to value and respect. As a white woman he is given everything he wants when he is angry, since his position in society entitles him to all the respect in the world. As a Black man, his anger is undeserved and treated as a danger.

In the next scene, Bruce goes downstairs at 2 a.m. to tell his Black neighbors, who are having a party, to turn their music down. They refuse and tell him that he should just move to another building. When he says that he will get upset, they respond, "Go ahead, Cuz!" Bruce then transforms into an emboldened white woman. Only then do they tell him that they will turn the music down. Once again, his emotional responses and requests are respected only when he is a white woman, but not when he is a Black man.

The "Impossible Hulk" skit reminds us that the extent to which a person's anger will be taken seriously is often based on their racial identity. The uptake of the anger is connected to the value we think the person possesses. In a patriarchal, white-supremacist society we think that some lives matter more than others, and thus the anger of some people matters more than that of others. (This is yet another way in which, despite years of protesting, the slogan "Black Lives Matter" must be repeated.) This context leads us to take more seriously the anger of those whom we think matter more, and to think—if we are a member of a racially dominant group—that our own anger matters more than others'.

How is this connected to allyship? A white ally might think that his anger at racial injustice matters more than the anger of the Indigenous person who is experiencing injustice. When an ally thinks his anger matters more than others, this doesn't mean that he also thinks an Indigenous person's anger or life does not matter. But the angry ally is not in the clear because of this. An ally can still behave badly, even with their Lordean rage, if they think that *their* anger matters *more*. This is again due to the prioritization of his white perceptions of value—of himself and of others.

The rage renegade is likely to have arrived at the judgment from a hierarchal, evaluative framework. That is to say, he might think, perhaps unconsciously, that the lives of racialized minorities only matter because his whiteness has declared them to matter. He might think that his valuation of them matters more than their own valuation of themselves—and indeed it will be hard for him to *not* think this when his anger on their behalf is listened to, and acted upon so much more than their anger on their own behalf. (Just like the Impossible Hulk, his white anger has a very different effect than the anger of the Indigenous person's would, given the respect that our society assumes white people—and only white people—are due.) Since valuing is connected to anger, he might therefore think that his Lordean rage matters more than theirs. Given this claim, it would not be surprising if the ally came to value the lives of certain racialized folk because their lives were previously valued by other whites—thereby making them worthy candidates for him to ascribe value.

A rage renegade who thinks that his anger matters more than the anger of the oppressed can engage in a variety of destructive acts. He may focus more on how he and other rage renegades feel than how members of the oppressed group feel. Whether he realizes it or not, what would be most important to him is what white people—say, the other white people he is connected with on social media—are feeling in response to Indigenous peoples' experiences of racial violence and marginalization, rather than what Indigenous peoples—with whom he might not even have any personal ties—are feeling about their own experiences. (More about allyship and grandstanding shortly.) As a result, a rage renegade may chronicle or express his Lordean rage without any desire to give voice to how the marginalized are feeling. If an ally has a blog or podcast, he will only talk about his feelings of rage rather than interview a friend of color or provide an opportunity for his Arab American coworker to speak about her anger. When a person of color is reporting their Lordean rage, an ally might attempt to one-up her in the emotion department. Rather than listening to someone who has endured racial mistreatment firsthand, his focus will be on voicing his own anger. If a person is angry, the one-upper will report that he is *angrier.* If a person is angry due to a recent racial incident, the one-upper will report that he has *always* been angry.

What is morally problematic about this kind of ally behavior? Many things. First, a rage renegade who thinks that his rage matters more than the oppressed is likely to not see people of color as having inherent value. (If asked, he would say of course they do, but his actions betray an unjust attitude he likely does not detect in himself.) They only have value because whites have ascribed value to them. Or they only have value because whites agree with the ascription. This is not an act of resistance against white-supremacist claims. It is a kind of valuing that is very much rooted in white supremacy. A person who only thinks that Black people have value because his anger cosigns it or makes it so is an ally of the worst kind. This is because the very foundations of his allyship are built on a white-supremacist foundation. The transformative possibilities of his Lordean rage are also likely to be negatively impacted as a result.

Even if a white ally does not have the extreme, noninherent valuation beliefs we have seen, thinking that rage renegades' anger matters more than the anger of the oppressed is still harmful, because it communicates that white people's feelings are more important than those of racial minorities. This reifies a racial hierarchy that says that white emotions, judgments, and perceptions have more value than others simply because they are held by those who are white.

A way not to give into this tendency to think or at least communicate that white feelings matter more than the feelings of other groups is to give people of color space to express their rage. To give space means to decenter or take the focus off oneself, if one is white, and allow the vulnerable (nonwhites) to be seen and heard, and to put their rage front and center. (This is what the retired navy officer in Portland was modeling in his interview.) In order to do so, a person must be able to distinguish between *appropriating* and *amplifying* the Lordean rage of others, and choose the latter. This means sometimes suppressing the urge to let everyone know that even though you are white, you are angry on behalf of Blacks, for example, and instead being quiet so that Black folks can speak for themselves. For allies, this often proves to be easier said than done.

Appropriating the Lordean rage of others is quite similar to appropriating the culture of others (or at least the problematic forms of doing so). In cultural appropriation, a person from a dominant group performs the art form associated with a culture that is not their own—one that enjoys less privilege—and, often, does not give credit to the group from which they have appropriated.[19] (As with rage, often the white person who has appropriated culture meets a different, more positive response for their use of the cultural object than the culture they are taking from would have, had they conveyed it themselves.) When a rage renegade appropriates the Lordean rage of others, she uses her rage in a way that fails to address the sufferings of nonwhites—which is the source of the rage. The rage becomes about her feelings, her experiences, her worries. She may also aim to gain attention for her rage and may receive it, while ignoring the fact that people of color are also outraged, and that their voices, feelings, and testimonies could get more attention if she got out of the way. This is an example of what Mychal Denzel Smith means by using allyship as self-congratulatory, a career, and as a way of centering one's own experience at the expense of the marginalized.[20]

Amplifying the Lordean rage of others is different from appropriating it. Amplification entails letting anger speak of the unjust conditions of others and not one's own situation, decentering oneself, and providing a platform for the marginalized to speak. This form of allyship is effective and does right by the Lordean rage of the oppressed. It may also include moving to the back of the line during a protest, refusing to sign your name first on a petition, or declining to speak on a racism panel and recommending a Black person instead. Amplifying the Lordean rage of others when we also have Lordean rage may be difficult to do since anger is so personal and we are the persons feeling it, evaluating the injustice, and being moved to do something about racism. This may also be hard to do since rage renegades are used to living in a society that prioritizes their experiences, perspectives, and feelings. However, allies must remember that even with passion, intensity, and good intentions, they could still participate in the silencing of vulnerable people's stories and experiences by making themselves and their anger the focus, thus communicating that their anger is more important. Rage renegades do not fight against racial discrimination and white supremacy when they do this. They contribute to racial injustice instead.

Moral Anger Grandstanding

An ally can also behave badly with their Lordean rage when using their rage performatively, to show off how virtuous they are, in a practice that has been called "moral grandstanding." In the context of Lordean rage, a person who participates in moral grandstanding uses rage to project a positive image of himself. He uses his rage for self-promotion, aiming to make himself look "woke," rather than aiming at defeating racism by publicly expressing outrage at it. A person can perform moral grandstanding in various ways, but let's call this type "moral anger grandstanding."

Allies who participate in moral anger grandstanding do it because they want to be perceived as exceptionally moral and anti-racist, and they use their rage as evidence. They might exaggerate their emotions. Imagine them reporting, "I am sooo angry," or "I am beyond outraged," most likely on social media, where all can see and be impressed by their righteous anger. To bring attention to their own rage, allies might feign intense expressions of it or they might self-report their anger in order to get praise and acceptance. They might express how angry they are in front of people of color in order to stand out as a good white person, or they might announce publicly to their Latinx friends that they are often angry at racist immigration practices, so that their racial values and politics can be applauded.

My statements may sound cynical. To be clear, allies are not always making such proclamations insincerely. Rage renegades could in fact be expressing anger at racial injustice, and it could come from genuinely wanting to see things change, rather than only wanting to look a certain way. But undeniably, at least one of the moral anger grandstander's goals is to project an image that he is a good white person. His reasons for doing so are not necessarily to make the oppressed feel safe or secure, or to strengthen solidarity ties—after all, plenty of whites express what has been called "performative wokeness" for their all-white or 99 percent white Facebook friends or Twitter followers. Instead, the purpose of expressing his rage is to showcase his own morality.

How might this be harmful? Philosophers Justin Tosi and Brandon Warmke claim that *general* moral grandstanding—moral grandstanding where a person uses moral talk to project a certain image—contributes to polarization since making strong moral claims in order to outdo others can lead them to refuse to listen to people on the other side of the political aisle.[21] This kind of grandstanding can also devalue moral talk since people will be less apt to take moral conversations seriously.

But what about moral anger grandstanding? I think that moral anger grandstanding has different effects. As we have already seen, what is worrisome about the term "ally" is that those who refer to themselves as such are often concerned with using the label as a sort of certification.[22] They often identify themselves with the label without putting in the work involved. I also want to make a slightly different claim here concerning grandstanding. Rage renegades might be so concerned with being identified as someone who is angry at racial injustice that they do not take advantage of the rage's motivational and productive features. Projecting the image of the angry ally is often the sum result of their rage. It's not just that they are inactive; they are misusing the fuel features found in Lordean rage that I discuss in Chapter 3. Recall, Lordean rage provides the fuel of eagerness, optimism, and self-belief to motivate anti-racist action. When a rage renegade participates in moral anger grandstanding, the fuel of Lordean rage is being used for *identification* and not anti-racist action. This is a waste of energy.

When an ally uses Lordean rage to morally grandstand, she might also think that she is immune to criticism. Because she perceives that her Lordean rage makes her a good white person, she can become resistant to any kind of moral criticism.[23] If her South Asian classmate points out a racist action she has participated in or a racist attitude she might have expressed, the moral anger grandstander will think that the criticism is not fitting—since she cannot possibly be racist or engage in racist actions because, well, she has anti-racist anger. And she thinks this because she believes that the emotion exonerates her from any kind of wrongdoing. In her eyes, she is angry at racial injustice and therefore exceptional—and she needs you to believe this too! When a rage renegade thinks she is immune to criticism, then even when she is called out and held accountable, she is more likely to continue to engage in actions that are detrimental to the goals of the marginalized group and contribute to the perpetuation of injustice.[24]

While allies can do this without rage, renegade ragers are likely to go a step further. In response to the criticism, a rage renegade may use her Lordean rage to block the accusation of racism. She will have anger in response to the criticism since she will think that the criticism itself is perhaps racist or an instance of racial injustice, and she will be motivated by her anger to end the injustice. Imagine the Black friends of a rage renegade calling her out for her anti-Blackness or questioning her solidarity. In response, she then expresses anger by saying, "No, you're the racist," or "You're being divisive." This is likely to create a cycle—the rage renegade responds to the accusation with Lordean rage while her friends respond to the original racist act or attitude with Lordean rage. The racial behavior is unlikely to be corrected, and those who are affected are unlikely to be heard as a result.

Moral anger grandstanding is also harmful when a person thinks that his anti-racist anger makes him morally superior to other whites and even other members of the oppressed group whose anger is not as present, strong, or loud as his. A rage renegade might think that because he has Lordean rage, he is therefore morally better than others. This might lead him to feel contempt for them. It might also create a self-designed moral hierarchy in which he judges and ranks everyone else's emotions and thus their morality. For example, a rage renegade may think that he is morally better than "those other white liberals" who do not have Lordean rage. He might even think that he is more virtuous or even "Blacker" than the Black person who fails to meet his level of anger. He may then begin to look at them with scorn or disrespect since their rage does not match his own. He may even judge them as morally inferior, insufficiently involved in democracy, uninformed and unaffected by suffering, and thus lower on the moral and political ladder. Beyond just being unfair to others, developing these attitudes could distract him from what should be the goal: combating racism. While having Lordean rage may signal an attunement to injustice, a certain moral judgment, and a just, inclusive perspective, it does not signal moral superiority.

This is morally problematic particularly since the construction of moral hierarchies is a strategy that racists often use in projects of racial domination. In these projects, they view certain people as morally superior and others as morally inferior. They create hierarchies based on this categorization. They also justify treatment and mistreatment, protection and elimination based on the moral hierarchy.[25] Holding contempt and creating hierarchies—although of a different nature than racists—are examples of how renegade raging can lead to reinforcing strategies and projects of racial domination rather than resisting them.

White Saviorism to the Rescue

Veronica Ivy argues that one thing that we expect allies to do is to use their social position to help the group with which they are in solidarity.[26] An example of this is when a white man uses his leadership position to hire minorities or when a white woman uses her white privilege to challenge the police who racially profile Latinx teens in her Brooklyn neighborhood. Another example is when white women protestors use their bodies as shields to protect Black protestors from the police, as they did in the 2020 Louisville, Kentucky, protests calling for justice in the death of Breonna Taylor.[27] But I think in some ways allies can use their social position to an extreme. White saviorism is an example of such an extreme, and an additional way that allies behave badly with their anti-racist anger.

White saviorism is "service" acts by members of a dominant group who think that other racial groups of people need saving and that only they can save them.[28] What also separates these service acts from pure acts of solidarity is that white saviorism centers the morality of whites. It is also about having a big emotional experience—the good feeling of protesting to get something off your chest—rather than about ending injustice. Lastly, those who engage in white saviorism tend to help nonwhites in self-serving ways and view them as helpless. Let's address each of these in turn to see how they can play out in Lordean rage.

An ally can use anger at racism to center the morality of white folks. By centering this morality, the focus of the anti-racist anger becomes about the goodness of white people rather than about addressing and ending the injustice that brought about the rage.

A satirical example of this is illuminating. In a 2019 spoof (on NBC's *Late Night with Seth Myers*) titled "White Savior: The Movie Trailer," comedian Seth Myers plays every white savior archetype in movies such as the *Green Book* and *Hidden Figures*. And his anger at racism is in the service of showing his Black friend the goodness of white people despite the existence of a "few" racist and prejudiced ones. Each scene riffs on a movie set in the Jim Crow South. When he expresses anger at white women for being appalled that his Black friend (played by Amber Ruffin) is using the "Whites Only" bathroom, at white men for intimidating her in a bar, and at a white man for being overly aggressive toward her, Meyers's character does it to illustrate just how good white people can be. He doesn't do it to challenge systematic racism or criticize his white friends' racist views. His first lines in the spoof, spoken at a press conference, sum up his intensions perfectly. As he adjusts the mic of his accomplished Black friend, who achieved some success *despite* racism, he takes attention away from her moment and seeks attention for his own goodness instead. "Her mic was too high, but I fixed it. It's fixed because of me," he says. In other words, rather than focusing on systemic issues or racist policies, he is focused on getting credit for being her savior.

Although using Lordean rage to center the morality of whites is similar to moral anger grandstanding, it is also quite different. A member of a racially dominant group who has Lordean rage and participates in white saviorism can use that rage to show how good, empathetic, and rebellious white people are. "Not all of them are racist!" is something they might attempt to prove. The focus of this morality is not necessarily themselves as individuals (as in the case of grandstanding) but white people in general. Their rage serves to redeem and center whiteness. The traits of goodness and empathy that emanate from whiteness are what the rage begins to represent. Centering the morality of whites turns Lordean rage into a badge of white honor. When one person wears the badge, he stands in proxy for many other whites—at least that is the thought.

When the focus becomes all about the rage that good white people have against racism rather than the racism that needs to be fought against, then injustice gets ignored. This misdirected focus gets in the way of the productive features of Lordean rage. It will be difficult for rage to lead to positive action that improves the lives of the vulnerable when injustice is ignored. Whites who have Lordean rage do not make up for or replace a white person who has hatred for Blacks. A rage renegade's actions do not erase the history of US racism. An ally with Lordean rage who thinks it does is engaging in a magical redemption project. The aim of anti-racist anger is to end racism, not erase negative images of whiteness. If that so happens to be a consequence, fine. But to make it a part of one's aim is not only likely to be a futile endeavor, but a distracting one, to say the least.

Centering the morality of whites also undermines what Lordean rage is all about. Lordean rage is a response to racism. It is not a representation of white morality. If this point is forgotten, then allies could end up participating in the erasure of people's experiences and neglect the task of addressing racist structures. This gets in the way of the ultimate aim of the rage—a radical transformation of our world.

White saviorism is not only about centering white morality but it also involves prioritizing white allies' angry emotional experiences. An ally can behave badly with Lordean rage at a racial protest, for example, in order to express or relieve themselves of their rage rather than, for example, pressuring local police chiefs to make anti-racist reforms. Afterward they might report, "That felt good," or "I feel better." This is not bad in itself. However, problems occur when people engage in protest only to make themselves feel better (i.e., express or release their rage) rather than fight to end injustice. Although justice is the aim of their Lordean rage, these renegades do not engage in actions to ensure that justice is achieved. Rather, justice-related efforts are merely aimed at providing a space for their "big emotional experience."[29] Rage renegades might think that their flourishing as community members may not directly depend on racial justice being achieved, and so having a big emotional moment or a grand cathartic experience often becomes sufficient for them. When the protest is over, they go home and move on to thinking about other things, not having effected change for those who don't get to stop thinking about racial oppression, since it constrains and defines their daily lives.

This is white privilege at its best—which is to say, at its worst. Whites may be able to rest after they express or release their anger. People of color, on the other hand, often cannot. Even if the Lordean rage of the racially marginalized subsides through expressive actions, racist oppression is still alive and ongoing—and thus the fight continues. When big emotional experiences become sufficient for rage renegades, this shows, among other things, an insensitivity to the lived experiences of the racially oppressed.

Lastly, those who engage in white saviorism through rage may tend to view nonwhites as helpless—so helpless that the white ally does not think that nonwhites can get freedom without their help. Because the allies' help is thought to be necessary, they might think that their anger is required for the freedom of oppressed people. This is different from thinking their anger matters more. It suggests, from an instrumental point of view, that allies' Lordean rage—and not the anger of the oppressed—is what is *necessary* for freedom.

White allies who think this way deny agency to nonwhites. By thinking this way, they refuse to see racial minorities as agents who can resist racial rules or be productive with their rage. By falling prey to white saviorism, allies reduce nonwhites to emotional beings whose anger cannot do anything in the world without white people's help and support. This view is hardly rooted in racial equality, even if racial equality is the ostensible goal. It's an irony that plagues the efforts of some of even the most self-professedly well-intentioned allies to the anti-racist cause.

Luckily for all of us, nonwhites can indeed fight for racial justice for themselves. My argument about the nature of and the possibilities for Lordean rage does not depend on whiteness to show up in order to make it so. Nonwhites can resist racial rules without whites sharing in the anger. Lordean rage is fitting and motivational even if whites never experience it. Rage renegades would do well to remember that while they can have particular roles in the anti-racist struggle (e.g., engaging in the epistemic labor of educating family members and challenging racist actions of those close to them) and their participation can add something to the fight for change, liberation does not depend on their presence. It takes humility to accept this. It also takes a constant shedding of racist ideology—an ideology that we all have inherited in some way—to accept that racially marginalized individuals are not helpless and do not require whiteness to make their lives better.

* * *

In sum, rage renegades can do harm with their Lordean rage when they think that their same feelings equate to the same experiences of the racially marginalized and their anger matters more than that of the oppressed. They can also do harm with their rage when they engage in moral anger grandstanding and white saviorism. While an ally can behave badly in numerous other ways, as we have seen, there are unique harms they can enact through rage.

This critical analysis is important for the additional barriers to productive allyship it uncovers, and for how it reveals the often-invisible ways in which social positions can pollute even our most fitting and laudable emotional responses to injustice. Unquestionably, the presence of allies is a good thing overall for anti-racist struggle. But to properly harness the potential that these allies' goodwill and attention can bring, allies must tackle the barriers we have seen so that they can continue to participate in anti-racist efforts in ways that are productive rather than self-serving, distracting, or even counterproductive.

Engaging in anti-racist work is not easy. There are minds to change, ideologies to resist, and racist systems to challenge. But this is not to say that the enemy or greatest threat always comes from outside forces. Those who are angry at racism can also do great harm. If we are not honest about the ways in which this can occur, we will be unable to do the real work of achieving a more just world. All of us, not just allies, could use a course in anger management to help us better navigate what to do with anti-racist anger.

6

Anger Management

An Alternative View

"Anger management." Enter the term into a search engine and you are bound to encounter TED Talks, psychology articles, motivational videos, and comedy skits dedicated to it. A movie, TV series, and rap tour bear its name. Anger management sessions are peppered in movie scenes starring favorite disgruntled characters like Tyler Perry's Madea and *Bad Boys'* angry cop Marcus (remember how he repeats "whoosa" to calm himself down?). An episode of the popular talk show *Dr. Oz* once featured the doctor explaining the ways in which certain foods could be used to cure anger.[1] All of these diverse mainstream references to anger management use the phrase as a euphemism for moderating, if not eliminating, anger. If it's a manager, it's not a very tolerant one—it's the kind that simply fires unruly employees.

We need to look at anger management in a different way. Just as good management in the corporate world is not just about firing people but solving problems as they arise and making sure that systems run efficiently, workers bring value, and everyone is productive, anger management should help us make sure our anger—our Lordean rage—*remains* appropriate, motivational, productive, and resistant. In other words, it should be actual management, not just euphemistic management. Rather than eliminating anger, we should work through it, harness it, and use it to achieve positive ends. As we have seen, some anger *is* already appropriate and directed toward constructive ends, so managing it means making sure that it fulfills its potential—not extinguishing its flames.

What would an alternative anger management plan—one that involves Lordean rage—look like? We shall soon see. But first, it can help to look at other suggested anger management techniques.

Anger Management: From the Ancients to Hollywood

Anger management has a rich history. Before psychologists arrived on the professional scene in the late nineteenth century, it was the philosopher's job to make sense of and offer strategies for controlling our emotions, particularly anger. Ancient Western thinkers like Sextius and Seneca and ancient Eastern thinkers like the Buddhist sage Sāntideva all made important contributions, many centuries before the term "anger management" was coined. While their worlds were long ago and very different from our own, people still sought to achieve political health and psychic well-being, and needed expert guidance. Ancient techniques included various cognitive, behavioral, and distraction therapies that aimed at controlling angry behavior and even altering the feeling itself.[2]

Sextius advocates self-examination as a way to limit our anger. He advises that the angry look themselves in the mirror. The idea is if the angry person sees her expression and the expressive change it brought about, then she will not recognize herself, the anger will alarm her, and this will give her reason to stop being angry. Sextius also thinks a person's anger will cease or become less intense if the angry person knows she has to stand before a judge each night (herself). He therefore recommends daily self-examination. Before Sextius went to bed at night, he asked himself, "What vice have you resisted? What part of you is better?"[3] Seneca recommends avoidance. He suggests that we avoid professions, people, and physical weariness that can exaggerate and irritate our minds. Those who are easily angered are advised not to meddle in serious occupations that may arouse their ire. Instead, they should get "softened by reading poetry . . . and legendary history."[4]

Sāntideva thinks that anger functions to cause harm and aims to wound others. Thus, the best antidotes to anger are compassion, lovingkindness, patience, and gratitude. The thought is that remaining angry is impossible when a person is experiencing these other states. When a person is angry, for example, Sāntideva recommends that he think about what he is grateful for, in order to extinguish the anger.

Most of the ancient thinkers argue for anger elimination, and their anger control techniques are specific to that goal. Today, most psychologists take a moderate approach toward anger, and their techniques for managing it reflect this approach. Psychologists do not think that anger is always inappropriate or disproportionate, but their anger management techniques are directed at anger that fits those categories.

Psychologists may find that some clients' anger is misdirected. The goal of anger management then is to discover the roots of anger, its true target. Other times, anger is deemed inappropriate only when it becomes the emotional response to all situations. In this case, clients are said to lack an emotional range and are encouraged to identify when they feel sadness or anxiety instead. Psychologists may find that the client's anger is disproportionate. Because disproportionate anger often leads to destructive outcomes, the goal of anger management is to bring anger down to a level that prevents internal and external destruction.

Present-day anger management is greatly influenced by the work of Raymond Navoco.[5] Navoco placed great emphasis on anger's cognitive, somatic-affective, and behavioral components, and we see his techniques employed in anger management group therapy sessions.[6] This image of anger management group therapy—one that focuses on discovering the anger, examining it, and relaxing in order to reduce it—has been depicted in popular media.

Take, for instance, the 2003 movie *Anger Management* starring Jack Nicholson (therapist) and Adam Sandler (angry patient). In the movie's group therapy sessions, we witness Navoco's anger management techniques play out. One particular scene begins with a patient (Lou) recalling the angry episode that led him to the group. He relives the recent angry experience by acting it out. Nicholson's character then explores the harmful effects of anger by asking Lou, "How did you feel you handled that situation?" Lou responds, "Not as well as I could've." The therapist then brings attention to a patient (Nate) who is listening to a basketball game through his headset. "Didn't we decide you shouldn't listen to the ball game?" Nicholson asks, reminding them all of the need for and their commitment to avoiding anger triggers. "It's just a regular-season game, not all that important," says Nate. Immediately after, Nate announces, "The anger sharks are swimming in my head!" Nicholson calms Nate down by getting him to chant a word that Alaskan Natives use to soothe their children—a relaxation tool to control the patient's arousal. When another patient (Chuck) starts to get angry and assumes a fighting stance in front of Sandler's character, Nicholson asks, "Is it worth going back to the penitentiary?" Chuck then stops, crediting the calming word as the reason for his defeat over anger— proving that he is indeed a "fury fighter."[7] This fictional example of Navoco's approach shows a combination of avoidance, distraction, and reminder techniques.

One need not attend an anger management program in order to control anger. Psychologists, neuroscientists, and religious leaders have all suggested personal techniques that an angry individual can use. The American Psychological Association recommends to, when angry, "breathe deeply, from your diaphragm. Slowly repeat a calm word or phrase such as 'relax' or 'take it easy.'"[8] This calmness practice is similar to Seneca's suggestion that we engage in activities to "soothe unhealthy minds." Sports psychologist John F. Murray recommends, "When anger is overwhelming you, do anything to break the pattern: tie your shoelaces, count to ten, write a letter to your grandmother."[9] This distraction technique is similar to the Stoic philosopher Anthendorus's recommendation to recite all the letters of the alphabet as soon as we become angry.[10]

Present-day cognitive emotional regulation also includes meditation. Alexander Fennel and colleagues found that a meditation session can reduce the body's response to anger.[11] They observed that when participants' anger was induced, those new to meditation were able to relax their heart rate, blood pressure, and breathing rates after their first meditation training. For experienced meditators, they were able to relax prior to and after meditation. Although Seneca did not have the science to back it up, perhaps this is why he admonishes us to "turn all of its [anger's] indications into their opposites: the face should be relaxed, the voice gentler, and the pace slower. Little by little, the externals will be matched with an internal formation."[12] This is not just a game of fake it until you make it. Although it is not meditation proper, Seneca saw that by relaxing our face, voice, and pace, something also happened on the inside. Unbeknownst to him, blood pressure was decreasing as the anger was also.

Responding to History: The Good, the Bad, and the Ugly

For over two thousand years, we have had resources—given to us by philosophers and psychologists—to help us control anger. That is the good news. But there is also bad news—at least for our purposes.

First, the techniques of ancient thinkers and contemporary psychologists apply more to proportionality and less to the appropriate, motivational, productive, and resistant features of Lordean rage. If the goal is to moderate anger, the techniques overwhelmingly help anger become moderate so that it can be more proportional to a given situation, for example, something minor that we are overreacting to—say, oversized road rage at the end of a hard day. Moderation, however, is not synonymous with appropriateness, motivation, productivity, or resistance. Moderation is about proportionality. A call for moderating anger assumes you're already "too" angry. Proportionality is about the "sort or level of angry response that is required."[13] The techniques discussed earlier overwhelmingly help anger's proportionality at the neglect of anger's other features. Sometimes we have very good reason to be angry—just as angry as we are—and attempts to "manage" that anger by lessening it would be a mistake.

The relaxation techniques that some advocate to help manage anger do assist with bringing anger down to a certain level—making sure that it is not too much. The avoidance technique of setting nothing before our anger that will make it grow helps us keep our anger at a certain level. The self-examination techniques of looking in the mirror, asking ourselves questions each night, or meditating may remind us of our angry behavior and the need to keep that behavior in check. However, keeping our angry behavior in check is not the same as indulging in productive behavior. All of these techniques help with the goal of proportionality, a standard that I argue in Chapter 2 is not relevant in assessments of appropriateness. Although the goal is worthwhile, the techniques have little to say to help anger become or stay appropriate, motivational, or resistant.

Not only do existing anger management techniques not address the features of anger that can make it an effective force for good, as we have been learning about throughout this book, the standard techniques may also get in the way of these features. If we are reminded of how harmful anger is, we may be too fearful or careful to the point of inaction in order to not arouse great horror. If we put the avoidance technique in practice as a rule and stay away from all things that make us angry, I am not sure we would ever approach a problem or be productive in bringing an end to racial injustice. We would always avoid or hide instead. If we employ the distraction technique it may succeed at recentering our focus away from serious issues like the racial wealth gap, Islamophobia, or misogynoir. While ignorance is bliss, political and social ignorance can have horrible consequences. Moreover, it bears stressing that those who bear the brunt of racism and oppression most directly don't get the luxury of ignoring these problems, peaceful as it might be to spend a day without worrying about them.

Lastly, the time-tested anger management techniques we have seen are more fitting for interpersonal and short-term rather than political and long-term contexts. For example, it is fairly easy to avoid a person in our private lives who makes us angry. We can stop going to social events where the person is likely to be. However, we cannot avoid political exchanges, racist policies, racial injustices, or other political and social factors and the actors who arouse our

Lordean rage. They are ubiquitous in ways that one or two people are not. While Seneca suggests that we avoid serious occupations if we are quick to anger, we cannot avoid being part of a polity or members of a community unless we leave political society. Although Seneca thought that some things are out of our control, so why get angry anyway, this pragmatic dimension has social justice implications that, in the context of racial injustice, are difficult to accept. Although racism may be out of one's control, striving to end racism and racist policies is within our control. And if anger helps with this end, it is useful.

Things would be ugly if there wasn't an alternative anger management plan. We need a plan that can speak to the aforementioned concerns—helping Lordean rage maintain its appropriate, motivational, productive, and resistant features.

An Alternative Plan

My alternative plan consists of four techniques and focuses specifically on Lordean rage and not anger in general. Although these techniques look drastically different in type and kind from the approaches discussed so far, they are, nevertheless, effective behavioral and cognitive techniques to help manage Lordean rage in ways that do not eliminate or reduce it but make use of its features, thereby helping it to perform its role in the anti-racist struggle. Rather than managing Lordean rage by extinguishing it, I suggest we manage anti-racist anger by cultivating it, so that it can be used for good.

The Expression Technique

It may seem too simple, but one way to manage Lordean rage is to express it. Let it out!

To *express* Lordean rage means to show, manifest, or reveal it. Expression, according to philosopher Sue Campbell, is "the public articulation or discrimination of our psychological lives through language and behavior."[14] Everything expressed must have a medium. There are myriad ways to express anger at racism. Anger—like other emotions—can be expressed through facial expressions, anger's canvas. People show anger with tight lips, lowered eyebrows, flared nostrils, or the blank-faced "silent treatment," among other ways. People can express Lordean rage through confessional statements such as, "I am angry," or "This racist world makes me very angry." And just as people have spoken, written, sung, and painted about love—just to name some of the most common expressions—so too have they captured their feelings of rage in many forms throughout the ages. They can make sure their angry words survive the moment, capturing them in writing as James Baldwin did in his late essays, or as Dante did long before him, when his *Divine Comedy* expressed his own rage about what his hometown, Florence—the city that exiled him—had become. Or they can set their angry words to a beat. Rap group Public Enemy's "Fight The Power" gives voice to injustices and the need to fight against them.[15] Singer Lauryn Hill's "Black Rage" calls out the historical civic neglect and physical death of Black bodies.[16]

When dealing with anger—specifically Lordean rage—by expressing it, we harness its power to bring about positive change. Not only is this a good idea because of the way it allows us to combat racial injustice, but it is good because it helps us avoid the dangerous pitfalls of keeping our anger to ourselves. While many of us—especially people of color—feel social pressure not to express anger, as we'll see, keeping it in is not the answer.

In "Uses of Anger" Audre Lorde writes, "I cannot hide my anger to spare your guilt, nor hurt feelings ... for to do so insults and trivializes all our efforts."[17] Here Lorde helps us see that not expressing anger at racial injustice, *in some contexts*, can downplay the wrongdoing, what's at stake, and the actions required to fix it. This is because unexpressed anger can communicate that there is nothing to be angry about or that a certain wrongdoing is not "so bad" that it would require our anger. In doing so, unexpressed Lordean rage is likely to downplay the values that are compromised or the future harms that may occur due to the wrongdoing. If the wrongdoing is not bad or not so bad, perhaps the harms that occur as a result aren't either. And if this is the case, then it does not make sense to work toward change.

But expressed Lordean rage affirms its appropriateness. It says that despite the risk of others' misunderstandings or even their discomfort, something has gone wrong in the world and anger is the fitting response to it. The situation is so serious that it calls for anger. Expressing anger is not just an act where anger announces its presence. It also proclaims that—given what has occurred—it has a right to be here.

The expression technique not only responds to the appropriate feature of Lordean rage, but it also aids the outraged in being productive. First, it helps a person be productive in contributing to her overall health. When Lorde proclaims that her response to racism is anger, she also explains what unexpressed anger has done to her. It has "eaten clefts into my living only when it remained unspoken," she writes. Quoting her daughter's words about silence at length in her essay "Eye to Eye," Lorde explains what happens when we keep Lordean rage unexpressed. "You're never really a whole person if you remain silent, because there's always that one little piece inside you that wants to be spoken out, and if you keep ignoring it, it gets madder and madder. . . . If you don't speak it out . . . it will jump up and punch you in the mouth from the inside."[18] Empirical research backs up this claim; repressing anger can increase stress.[19] Since repression of emotions is also linked to the suppression of the body's immunity system, psychologist James Pennebaker argues that those who repress their anger are vulnerable to certain illnesses.[20] This all shows just how clearly self-destructive unexpressed anger is.

Second, expressing Lordean rage helps us be productive in contributing to the overall health of our society. If unexpressed anger keeps us silent and passive instead of active in making unhealthy conditions healthy, then this explains why expressed anger, as Lorde sees it, is liberating. As she famously puts it, "Your silence will not protect you."[21] Lorde is warning us about a silence not only of verbal but emotional speech. Unexpressed anger does not protect us because as long as it is silent, it is useless. Only when it is expressed in some form can we use it in the pursuit of justice and liberation.

Expressing anger also saves Lordean rage from being counterproductive. This is because unexpressed anger can, in some contexts, be destructive.

For James Baldwin, consciously living with anger requires us to avoid useless anger. And anger is only useless for Baldwin when it is unexpressed and contains hate. In *A Talk to Teachers,* he states,

> What I am trying to get at is that by this time the Negro child at this point [a teenager who has grown up in a racist country] has had, effectively, almost all the doors of opportunity slammed in his face, and there are very few things he can do about it. He can more or less accept it with an absolutely inarticulate and dangerous rage inside—all the more dangerous because it is never expressed. It is precisely those silent people whom white people see every day of their lives—I mean your porter and your maid. . . . They really hate you—really hate you because in their eyes (and they're right) you stand between them and life.[22]

Anger is only destructive for Baldwin when it is unexpressed. This should be avoided. But he also thought that unexpressed anger turns into bitterness—a prolonged anger that transforms to hate (self-hatred and hatred for whites). Baldwin recognized that this hatred not only destroys the person because it has a "murderous power over you" and leaves you in a "self-destroying limbo"—but it may lead you to destroy others.[23] Is there a way to take hate-based anger in a specific moment and funnel it into anger at wider social conditions, in a way that makes that anger the fuel for positive change? I think so. As discussed in Chapter 1, the types of anger that arise in the context of racial injustice (rogue, narcissistic, wipe, ressentiment, and Lordean rage) can run into each other. A person's wipe rage can transform into Lordean rage, perhaps, if the hatred is redirected from vicious people to vice. In this way, a person begins to hate racism instead of racists. And they are more likely to be motivated to eliminate racism rather than racist people.

Lorde also thought that a person's unexpressed anger could *hurt* other people. We often direct our bottled-up emotions at people who are close to us. If we are racially marginalized or in solidarity with the oppressed, they are likely to be our targets. The real target escapes our anger, and the real problem is never addressed. Lorde witnessed this with her white allies. She writes, "I have seen situations where white women hear a racist remark [against Blacks] . . . become filled with fury, and remain silent, because they are afraid. That unexpressed anger lies within them like an undetonated device, usually to be hurled at the first woman of Color who talks about racism."[24] These white women have anger at racism. However, their anger is often unexpressed to its proper target. Perhaps the women are afraid of what they might lose as a result, so they keep it bottled up. But remember, bottled-up emotions in one context are likely to spill out into aggressive actions in another. In interracial feminist communities, Lorde is noting how the unexpressed anger of white women—even at racism—can spill into aggressive acts and attitudes directed at Black women—women who don't need or deserve such behavior.

The idea here is not that Lordean rage should be expressed outwardly, in the conventional sense, to any and every one and at all times. There may be reasons to keep it unexpressed. Unexpressed anger may help an angry person to protect themselves from retaliation, rejection, or the adverse reaction of powerful opponents. Not expressing the emotion can give her time to think before she says something rash and save her from the regret that might follow doing something hurtful that she can't take back. Not expressing one's anger can also help bystanders by sparing them an uncomfortable scene, as well as the person at whom the anger is directed, of course. These considerations might be outweighed in many contexts. For Baldwin, life-and-death situations were instances in which keeping anger unexpressed was wise—but short of that, it was important to express anger. This is not to say that expressed anger is always destructive. Nor is it to say that expressing anger defiantly when your life is on the line is the only way to demonstrate Lordean rage. But if you're in a situation where the stakes are existentially high, how far is too far to go when expressing rage?

Let's address the (angry) elephant in the room: violent expressions.[25] Defenders of anger often choose to separate *being* angry and *behaving* angrily in their analysis and they dedicate most of their theorizing to the former. This can be read as a subtle way of ignoring the elephant. One of the worries of the ancients and many contemporary anger critics is violent expressions of anger. They are worried that the expressive tendency of anger is violence. Just as Seneca cited historical events as proof of anger's destructive nature, critics today may cite the 1992 Los Angeles riots, 2015 Baltimore uprising, or the small percentage of protestors in 2020 who looted stores and destroyed property as more recent examples of violent expressions of anger at racial injustices.[26] In Chapter 1, I argued how and why other types of anger (and not Lordean rage) are prone to express themselves violently. But here it's worth returning to the "violent expressive" worry because the expression technique plays an important role in minimizing violence rather than contributing to it.

As I mentioned, there are a variety of ways to express anger. One of those expressions can be violence, but it is not *the* action tendency of anger. Violence can become an expression of anger when anger is otherwise not expressed or unaddressed. It is usually the last resort, but can be avoided if we find a more productive outlet before we get so desperate that we go there. One way of responding to the fear that expressing anger will lead to violent uprisings, for example, is to say that the participants always felt anger, they just never expressed it. Violence is not what happens when you express anger but when you keep it in, causing it to reach a boil and then explode. Or when you don't acknowledge it when it's there, as is the case with repression. In this sense, suppressing anger until it can no longer be shut out is likely to lead to violence, but this is not an expression problem. It is a repression and [extreme] suppression problem. For example, scientists from the University of Texas at Austin and the University of Minnesota have conducted studies that conclude that suppressed emotions lead to aggression.[27] They argue that people who bottle up their emotions in one situation (e.g., at work) are more likely to act aggressively afterward (e.g., at home).

People are also likely to suppress their anger and ultimately resort to violent expressions when expressive resources—avenues and ways to express anger—are limited. Resources can be town hall meetings, protest marches, voting, social media platforms, art, organizing activities, and so on. If citizens do not have access to these resources, they may see violence as a last and only expressive resort. If "riots are the language of the unheard," as Martin Luther King Jr. once claimed, then we must figure out how to ensure that angry people have ways to express their anger.[28] If we rob individuals of expressive resources, they are more likely to show anger in violent ways since violence is a natural resource. By "natural resource" here, I mean that it doesn't require much for us to make use of it, and it's always there, like air. Even if an angry person is isolated from others, they can hurt themselves. If put in a straitjacket, a person can still bite their lips. If you don't have any weapons, you can still punch, shove, and kick. Dogs, who are very much dependent on humans for survival due to domestication, can be independent when it comes to violence—they can bite. This is how "natural" violence is as a resource.

We rob others of expressive resources when we disenfranchise them, block them from demonstrating, wave guns at them while they peacefully protest, dictate to them unfair expressive standards (more on this ahead), deny them access to media and cultural expressions, and more. King observed that "the Negro has many pent-up resentments and latent frustrations and he must release them."[29] For this reason, King demands that they be granted expressive resources when he writes, "Let him march; let him make prayer pilgrimages to the city hall; let him go on freedom rides." But he also issues a warning: "If his repressed emotions are not released in nonviolent ways, they will seek expression through violence; this is not a threat but a fact of history."[30] The focus should not be on attacking any and all expressions of rage. Instead, we should ensure that we all have access to a variety of expressions so that violence is not the default anger expression. To be clear, I am not suggesting that violence is never justified. I am persuaded by arguments from political philosophers such as Candice Delmas who claim that civil disobedience is not the only kind of principled disobedience. It also includes uncivil disobedience, which may comprise some forms of violence.[31] I am simply arguing that violence is not the only form of expression for the outraged.

The Solidarity Technique

After Lordean rage has been expressed, how can this anger be translated into productive action? Expression is a first step, but it is not sufficient. A way to get there is the solidarity technique, which entails getting connected with others who can provide mutual support and community. One of the benefits of the expression technique is that it helps with this aim. Expression reveals with whom one can be in solidarity. "For it is in the painful process of this translation," Lorde writes, "that we identify who are our allies with whom we have grave differences, and who are our genuine enemies."[32] When you express anger at injustice you can—by the responses and reactions of others—discover who are those you can be in solidarity with and those from whom you should stay clear. If others listen to you despite the differences between you, they are allies. If they silence you, they are enemies. If they take you seriously, they are allies. If they immediately dismiss you, they are enemies. Expressing Lordean rage can reveal your true friends.

The solidarity technique is an anger management technique for several reasons. Solidarity provides the support needed to validate Lordean rage's appropriateness. Being angry alone is isolating. When you are alone you are more likely to doubt that you have a reason to be angry because no one is around to validate your right to be angry. In solidaristic spaces, validation occurs by empathizing and letting others know that they are not wrong in feeling their anger. When problems are systematic, it is important to know that others feel the way you do or that they understand such feelings. Being in solidarity with others is a way to receive and provide this supportive validation. The solidarity is a reminder that your Lordean rage is an appropriate response to racial wrongdoing. This is essential to recognize if one is to use this same rage in pursuit of social and political ends.

The solidarity technique is also an anger management technique because, in connecting us with others who share common goals, it provides moral critics to help us monitor anger's productivity. The solidarity technique provides a trusted community that people can rely on to challenge them and hold them accountable in their anger.

If at any point anger becomes unproductive, a moral critic can point it out. At any point that anger becomes inappropriate, you can help others correct it. Being in solidarity with others is not a euphemism for being at a rage fest—a place where people come together only to get more angry. Nor is it meant to encourage folks to gang up on their common enemy online. Instead, it provides a space to challenge each other's Lordean rage in constructive ways so that it maintains its productive and resistant features.[33]

The purpose of the solidarity technique is not to alert you to anger so that you can get rid of it. You should keep this anger since it has an important role to play in anti-racist struggle. The solidarity technique instead allows for critics in the form of a trusted community to alert you only when you are being unproductive with your anger.

Also, the community critics we find in solidaristic spaces are not just wise and disciplined. They are people with whom you are in solidarity, which matters for the kind of feedback you need. In other work I argue that we face limitations and errors in evaluating the political anger of others.[34] We are not always familiar with the cause of other people's anger. Injustices can have proximate causes (e.g., the shooting death of Breonna Taylor) and historical causes (e.g., the history of police violence). If a critic is unfamiliar with these causes—either because they do not know anyone who suffers from them or they refuse to believe that they exist—they are likely to judge the anger incorrectly, because the information that is needed to adequately judge the anger, at least immediately, is missing. However, a person with whom we are in solidarity is likely to already have this information, so they are more likely to judge our anger correctly. But there is another limitation for the "outsider" critic. It's hard to understand people's anger the more distant you are from them. I refer to this as the sympathy gap. We are more likely to sympathize with the anger of those close to us than those far away. When we live far from disenfranchised communities or have only one Black friend, we are more likely to fail at imagining ourselves in their shoes in order to understand and thus judge their anger correctly. Also, there's a chance that outside critics are more likely to participate in discursive social practices—intentionally or unintentionally—such as anger policing and gaslighting as a result. In order to protect the outraged from these inaccurate assessments and the harms that may occur, the solidarity technique allows for only the wise and disciplined person *with whom we are in solidarity* to serve as our critics.

The solidarity technique also helps with the motivational feature of Lordean rage. Being in solidarity with others can motivate the angry even more to struggle against racism, because motivation is contagious. In a study at the University of Rochester, Ron Friedman and colleagues came to this conclusion by conducting a series of experiments in which employees were put into rooms with other colleagues.[35] Researchers found that simply placing an employee in the same room with a highly motivated colleague enhanced their performance. Researchers refer to this unconscious mimicking of the motivation of others as *motivational synchronicity*. It is not something we develop when we enter the workplace. We are born this way. Motivational synchronicity has the evolutionary benefits of allowing us to bond and share resources. If Lordean rage is motivational, as I argue in Chapter 3, then being around other angry people feeds one's own motivation. This motivation contagion allows people not only to bond with community members but also helps them work together for change since motivation can enhance performance.

This technique can also help fuel the motivational aspect of anti-racist anger by serving as an antidote to protest and racial battle fatigue. Law professor Richard Thompson Ford defines *protest fatigue* as "a sense of weariness and cynicism about social protests and movements."[36] *Racial battle fatigue* occurs when Blacks, while fighting for justice, continue to experience the cumulative impacts of racism, are regularly bombarded with images depicting Black death, and find themselves constantly dealing with white allies in laborious ways. This fighting on multiple fronts creates exhaustion, induces guilt for wanting to take breaks from it all, and can lead people to neglect their well-being. This all results in burnout.[37] The solidarity technique is one antidote among many that can help with these forms of fatigue. A trusted community can provide the care needed to curb burnout. By sharing in emotional work, stepping in when others need to take a break, and providing consistent community care to others, the solidarity technique allows the community to take care of its outraged members so that they can live to fight another day. Some might only suggest self-care as an antidote to protest fatigue. But self-care is never done in isolation, as I've argued elsewhere.[38] Even when we are taking care of ourselves, someone is chipping in to make that possible. Someone is teaching the yoga class we attend, suggesting the music that can calm us down, and listening to us as we express our worries and concerns. With this kind of community care, we are likely to stay motivated to fight racism. Without it, we are more likely to burn out.

The Goals and Plans Technique

On March 13, 2020, Breonna Taylor, a Black twenty-six-year-old emergency medical technician and aspiring nurse, was gunned down by Louisville, Kentucky, police officers during a midnight no-knock warrant raid. Critics as well as the police chief responsible described the officers' actions as miscalculated, a "shock to the conscience" and displaying "an extreme indifference to the value of human life." People expressed Lordean rage. They marched in protest; placed Breonna on billboards and magazine covers; wore T-shirts that said, "Arrest the cops that killed Breonna Taylor"; and promoted the hashtag #JusticeForBreonna. Their goals were clear: bring awareness to her case and get her justice.

Creating goals and a plan to achieve them helps Lordean rage maintain its motivational and productive features. Researchers have found that setting goal targets increases motivation.[39] People are also more motivated to finish what they have set out to do when they are closer to achieving their goal. Setting goals then adds fuel to the motivational fire of Lordean rage. When you have clear goals as a person with Lordean rage, you are able to stay motivated to work to achieve them. In response to the case of Breonna Taylor, those with Lordean rage were able to stay motivated for months despite inaction from local authorities because they had goals in mind.

Goal setting is also an antidote to fatigue. Another source of protest fatigue is hopelessness. By constantly experiencing or witnessing racism—even as one works to combat it—a person with Lordean rage may begin to feel that all hope is lost, that racism will never die. However, setting goals, even short-term ones, and working to achieve them can sustain their hope and keep them motivated. Ending racism may be the ultimate aim but that won't happen today. Goals like raising awareness of racial mistreatment and getting justice for a young Black woman *can* be achieved today, however. Goals like these can help the outraged maintain their drive, even in disheartening times.

People work harder when goals are set, but plans provide road maps to achieve goals. They tell us what actions to take to get to change. In other words, they reveal how we might be productive. Without road maps we will not know what actions to take. Therefore, Lordean rage needs road maps in order to be productive and, ideally, effect change.

Lorde asserts that "anger expressed and translated *into action in the service of our vision and our future* is a liberating and strengthening act of clarification."[40] Anger translated *into action* is anger that is used to do work. *Vision* is what we imagine the world to be.[41] It is the goal one fights for. Without vision (goals), a person would not know what the end of her angry action is or to what purpose her anger should be put to use. Action fueled by anger follows a road map that leads to a realization of a vision of a better future. The goals and plans technique reveals what action Lordean rage should be engaged in to be productive and the goals toward which one's angry actions should strive.

The goals and plans technique also provides a way to assess if one's Lordean rage is productive. Although setting goals provides a framework for which one can be productive, the outraged person needs a way to judge if and when her rage is productive. Goals provide a set of standards. In this way we can judge anger's usefulness not after change has been achieved—which may take time, since for Lorde "change is a radical alteration in all those assumptions underlining our lives"—but when a short-term goal or plan of action has been accomplished.[42]

For example, if I set a goal for people to become aware of racial discrimination at immigration offices through my angry protest, then I know that my Lordean rage has been productive when, for example, I spread the message. If I do nothing with my rage by not addressing immigration, then I know that my anger has not been productive. Since anger is often unfairly judged to be unproductive by those judging from afar, as we have seen (people who are also often scared and resistant to the positive change the anger might ignite), this technique is important. It is important to have one's own set of assessment standards. Other people's standards of your rage's productivity may be based on how your anger makes them feel or if it does what they want it to do (although this does not preclude the same risk applying to my own standards). But having your own set of standards is important for helping you stay focused on the goals that matter to you.

A person angry about the shooting of Breonna Taylor can know if their anger is being productive if they are working their plan. Are they bringing awareness to her case? Are they demanding that the officers be brought to justice? Are they resisting feeling rules that say Black women are not worth our care? Are they doing their part to make sure that policies that made it legal for police to enter her home are changed? In the case of Taylor, the family received a financial settlement. Part of the settlement banned the use of no-knock warrants (called Breonna's Law), required body cameras during search warrants, and offered housing credit for officers who move to low-income neighborhoods they patrol. These outcomes resulted from the hard work of people who channeled their Lordean rage to effect change, through protest and other activism.

Results such as these are not promised. And it would be unfair to judge the anger's productivity based only on what it actually achieves rather than what it aims at achieving. Anti-racist struggle doesn't always end the way we expect. Sometimes we achieve progress, but other times we do not. When progress occurs, backlash often follows. It's a long battle. For example, soon after the settlement, only one officer out of three were indicted. Moreover, the officer who was indicted was not charged for Breonna's murder but only for putting her neighbors in harms' way. Nevertheless, having the goals to strive toward and working the plan to achieve them offer a good way to guide the outraged and to ensure they are being productive with their rage.

Resistance Technique

As we've already seen, critics are crucial to help us manage Lordean rage and to stay focused on our goal of defeating racism and racial injustice. Since we need the appropriate, motivational, productive, and resistant features of Lordean rage, it is important that outraged people do not allow others to persuade them to get rid of it prematurely. In other words, you must listen to others, but do so carefully. Silencers can try to pressure us to quit, to give up on the cause. If the outraged person does not develop the capacity to resist them, she will not be able to take advantage of all that is good about Lordean rage. So, in arming ourselves with all the techniques that help us cultivate productive Lordean rage, we have to learn how to resist those who seek to squelch it.

The first kind of silencer is the anger police. The anger police disapprove of anger not because of its features but because of its presence. They always look at Lordean rage as an inappropriate response to racial injustice. This is not to say that Galen and Seneca are part of the anger police because they judged anger to be inappropriate. There's more to the anger police profile than disapproval. The anger police also live by a double standard. We are likely to discover that although the anger police view the anger of others as inappropriate, they approve of their own anger and the anger of their racial group.

The anger police are also quite bossy. They want the outraged person to express her discontent on their terms. The anger police dictate the way the angry person should talk about her experiences and goals. They often suggest that if the angry person change her emotional state, then she will be heard. They also use certain standards of civility and rationality to dictate how, when, and why the outraged can speak. The goal of the anger police is to silence those with Lordean rage in an effort to not only assert their own power over them, but to minimize the transformative work that Lordean rage can do.[43]

How might someone with Lordean rage resist the anger police? They first can recognize the difference between the anger police and the moral critic in the solidaristic sense that I discussed earlier. The anger police may be a policing wolf in solidaristic clothing. Recall that one of the purposes of being in solidarity with others is to be held accountable. The community's role is to recognize when you are not being productive and to challenge you as a result. But this is not subjective. The standards from which they judge will be based on the goals and plans of the group or cause. The anger police's approach is quite different.

You can distinguish the anger police from moral critics by their standards of quietness, civility, comfort, or respectability. The problem with the anger police is not that they value these four standards, nor that they value them more highly than the goals of Lordean anger on some occasions. It is that even when these standards clearly ought to be overridden by something else of value, they would still give them priority. Why? Because by insisting on them, they can quiet voices that challenge the status quo that benefits them.

Another way of resisting the anger police is to always remember anger's usefulness. Lorde understood that "everything can be used, except what is wasteful." And she reminds readers that they "will need to remember this, when [they] are accused of destruction."[44] The anger police's tactics involve accusing Lordean rage of destruction, not production. This move works because it gets at the sensitivity of those who are outraged. They are angry because they are sensitive to racial injustice and the destruction that lies in its path. The last thing those with Lordean rage may aim to do is inflict harm on others. If the anger police are effective, they can get outraged people to be ashamed of their Lordean rage and therefore get rid of it. But an outraged person should remember that although anger is sometimes destructive, Lordean rage can also be useful.

Finally, one can resist the anger police by refusing to give up when she has no reason to do so. A person with Lordean rage may remember that her anger is useful, but she may give it up in order to avoid causing trouble or to make things easier.[45] Expressive strategies have a place when it comes to Lordean rage, but when the outraged person finds herself accommodating the anger police instead of strategizing, she is not resisting but giving in. To resist entails refusing to give up the anger, at least until there is reason to do so. Lorde recognizes that Black women in particular are often encouraged to be angry on other people's behalf, but never on behalf of themselves. When they are angry at injustices concerning themselves, they are asked to give up that anger. Lorde, writing in 1981, declared, "That time is over."[46] (Let us hope that, at least by now, these words are true!) This is an assertion of anger's appropriateness on behalf of Black women. It says that any violation or disrespect of Black women's lives is worth the anger. The statement is also the beginning of a claim of refusal.

Other silencers are also at work. Borrowing from the analysis of Sue Campbell, I refer to them as "anger dismissers." Anger dismissers do not name Lordean rage as the emotion one is feeling. Because they are likely to recognize the moral judgments the anger involves, the dismisser refuses to name the anger as anger. To name the anger as such is to acknowledge the racial wrongdoing that brought the anger about and thus the angry person's right to be angry. Naming the anger is also a way of respecting the angry person's claim that she or others matter. So, by refusing to name the anger—and instead, for example, saying that the anger is actually bitterness—the anger dismisser silences the angry person.

This is, of course, a distortion of the anger. The dismisser views the interests of the angry person as insignificant—for if they were significant, the dismisser would be more likely to see the outraged as reasonable and view their emotional response as appropriate. That is why dismissal is a clever strategic move. It takes agency away from the angry person by saying that they don't get to have power over articulating their emotions as they wish. It gaslights them, effectively telling them they are mistaken. In order to minimize and push the anger under the rug, the anger dismisser names the anger as something else—an emotion that is an easier target of disapproval.

Dismissing anger in this way can also be a way of blaming the angry for further racial disadvantages. The dismisser may suggest that the bitterness stands in the way of making progress. If they were not bitter, they would be able to change their situation. If they were not bitter, others would be willing to help. But because they are bitter, progress is not being made. This is not the fault of the system, the dismisser may argue. It is the fault of the emotional person. This is, of course, a form of victim blaming as well as a form of gaslighting.

The dismisser needs to feel a sense of power, and because they feel threatened by Lordean rage, they call it something else. The dismisser has to be right that it is bitterness, and he needs you to believe this. He might insincerely express that he cares about justice and believes the world is more racially just than it was in the 1960s, and for these reasons, your strong response to a racial incident is because "you are just bitter." But it could also be the case that the silencer dismisses Lordean rage as bitterness and, at the same time, actually thinks no further racial disadvantages remain. The latter case, in fact, is part of what explains why he characterizes Lordean rage as bitterness. In other words, you could actually dismiss anger at racial justice in good faith—say, if you're a white person who (somehow) doesn't think there is racial injustice to be fought—or you could do it in bad faith—trying to get an angry person to give up on their cause because you actually did perceive the injustice, but it worked for you (because you're of the dominant race). Regardless of good or bad faith, the gaslighter aims to create what psychologist Robin Stern refers to as the gaslight effect.[47]

Campbell gives us a solution. She suggests that dismissers be politically resisted. "Block the criticism instead of defending it."[48] However, Campbell doesn't explain further what blocking is or what it entails. Writing twenty years later, philosopher Rae Langton gives us some insight on this matter.[49] She uses this helpful example to ꞌring the idea to life. Say you are at baseball or basketball game and a spectator yells at a player and says that he is playing like a girl. This comment is misogynistic, on top of being meant to insult the male player. To compare the player to a girl in this way is to say that the player lacks ability. To block the criticism would entail a spectator saying, "What's wrong with being a girl?" In this way, the responder attempts to make the misogynistic comment lose its effect. In basketball, for example, a defensive player can block a player's shot. In blocking, they attempt to render the shot, although attempted, immaterial to the game. Similarly, in blocking a misogynistic comment, you make it lose its effect. You do this by rejecting the premise that playing like a girl would be a bad thing and not accommodating or helping the statement along by being silent or by saying "Yeah!" Instead, you block the statement with your words, as a defensive player would block a shot with their hands, so that you can prevent it from having a negative effect.

We can use the same blocking technique when it comes to anger dismissers. We can respond to their attempts to silence us by turning things back around on them: "What's wrong with bitterness?" or "Asian Americans have a right to be angry too!" But notice that this kind of blocking is only directed to the dismisser. What about the target of the comment? Shouldn't we also talk to them?

If we find ourselves bystanders in a situation like the sports event Langton describes, we could also block by talking to the target of the dismissal—not just the dismisser. We can be allies, providing solidarity for the person whose rage the dismisser aims to squelch by mischaracterizing it as what it is not. We can say to the outraged, "There is nothing wrong with the way you feel," or "They call it bitterness, but reasonable people call it anger," or simply, "Don't let them tell you what you're feeling right now." This, I think, is an effective way of resisting the anger dismisser. It bypasses the need for a constant back-and-forth between the dismisser and the angry person. It also saves the angry person from having to give anger dismissers attention when there is more important transformative work to do. And it also, in a nice way, pays it forward. We might need someone to support our rage some day!

Traditional anger management techniques fail to give proper attention to the appropriate, motivational, productive, and resistant features of Lordean anger, but, as we've now seen, alternative management techniques can support Lordean rage and help steer it through challenges.[50] Anger is not the scary monster that many believe it to be. It has an important role to play in anti-racist struggle. And it can play this role in very positive ways. It should not be eradicated. Instead, like a good manager, we should do what we can to help our anger do its very best to assist us in bringing about a more just world. It will not always be easy. But it will be worth it.

7

The End of Rage?

On April 28, 1973, a ten-year-old Black boy, Clifford Glover, was shot and killed by a white New York City police officer. The officer was indicted for his murder but eventually acquitted of charges by a jury of his peers (eleven of the twelve were white men). Audre Lorde heard the verdict on the radio while driving from the airport. "Sickened with fury, blinded by rage," writes her biographer, she pulled her car over.[1] On the side of the road she wrote a poem titled "Power":

> I am trapped on a desert of raw gunshot wounds
> and a dead child dragging his shattered black
> face off the edge of my sleep
> blood from his punctured cheeks and shoulders
> is the only liquid for miles

She continues,

> A policeman who shot down a ten year old in Queens
> stood over the boy with his cop shoes in childish blood. . . .
> this policeman said in his own defense
> "I didn't notice the size nor nothing else
> only the color."

Reflecting on her own agency and the future, she writes,

> I have not been able to touch the destruction
> within me.
> But unless I learn to use
> the difference between poetry and rhetoric

> my power too will run corrupt as poisonous mold
> or lie limp and useless as an unconnected wire.[2]

In this moment, Audre Lorde is faced with the reality of Black death at the hands of the police as well as the justice system's shameful and inadequate response to it. Nevertheless, she is trying to figure out how to use her own power and anger not to destroy or corrupt, but to wield it in useful ways. She is also reminding us of the power we all possess. In order to make use of this power, there are some things we must learn first.

The book you have in your hands was written on the proverbial side of the road. I wrote and revised it upon hearing about the raw gunshot wounds that pierced the Black skin of Trayvon Martin, Tamir Rice, Breonna Taylor, Michael Brown, and others—whose killers were never indicted, or when indicted, were acquitted. I wrote this on the side of the road as I attempted to make some sense of the mysterious and not so mysterious treatment of Sandra Bland and Freddie Gray in police custody, and Eric Garner and George Floyd in the police's deadly grip. I wrote this on the side of the road as the nation gasped and wept at the actions of a white supremacist who killed nine Black churchgoers who had only moments earlier welcomed him with a smile one summer evening in Charleston, South Carolina. I pulled over to write this book as I witnessed video footage and images of a white nationalist and a militia member kill anti-racist protestors, and politicians' and white citizens' attempt to justify it. While refusing to believe that nothing could be done to combat this racism and these injustices, I wrote and rewrote this book to figure out what was within me—us—and how we could use our own power through the simmering anger that was rising within us. Unsurprisingly, the thinker who was both an intellectual resource and a psychological rock was Audre Lorde.

Lorde was a poet, teacher, activist, and mother. The author of twelve books that span the genres of poetry, autobiography, and essay, her words have always pierced my heart and challenged my thinking. Audre Lorde's work has played a large part in how I view the world, its problems, and our own agency. I relate to her writings, as well as her life. Lorde was the darkest child in her family. I am too. She constantly felt out of place. I often do also. She minored in philosophy in college. I majored in it. She was a queer Black woman. I am as well. We taught at the same university and unapologetically wore our natural hair way before it became trendy in our respective eras. And she was constantly motivated to live up to her full potential as a writer and warrior. I share the same obsession.

While I cite her poetry, I first came to Lorde through her essays. You would not know it by reading, but writing prose was something of a struggle for her. The linear thinking it required as well as the nature and importance she gave to the work were reasons for the difficulties.[3] Although she rejected the label of theorist, I find theoretical jewels and practical importance in her essays each time I return to them. No other essay speaks more to me, speaks different things to me each time I reread it, than "Uses of Anger." This essay first inspired many of my philosophical questions and claims concerning anger.

In the summer of 1981, she delivered "Uses of Anger" as a speech at the National Women's Studies Association Convention on the theme "Women Respond to Racism." Lorde begins by defining racism, cites personal racist encounters, and then goes on to explore the nature and role of anger in it all. Some attendees were demoralized by the speech. They thought they had a bigger enemy to target—the patriarchy. Focusing on each other's failures and embracing anger in response to them could only be a distraction. But for Lorde, racism had to be faced no matter who it came from. The anger had to be explored and used. The essay was originally published in *Essence* magazine and inspired another essay on Black women's anger, titled "Eye to Eye: Black Women, Hatred, and Anger." "Every BLACK WOMAN in America lives her life somewhere along a wide curve of ancient and unexpressed angers," reads the opening line. It is a meditation on misogynoir, self-hatred, community, anger, and love. Both would be published with other essays in the collection *Sister Outsider*, which reviewers described as "an eye-opener" and its author as "a convincing, powerful writer."[4]

The racism that Lorde was concerned about in "Uses of Anger," and the racial actions that inspired the poem "Power," have not disappeared. Police brutality targeted against Black and Brown bodies persists some forty-seven years after the poem was penned. The racism that inspired "Uses of Anger" is still alive today. Lorde's work has never been more relevant.

Scholars often find joy in making connections. It can be exciting to discover similarities and detect relevance between what a writer wrote decades ago to what you, the scholar, is thinking about today. But as an African American philosopher, I am exhausted! As much as I've wrestled with Lorde's ideas on the page and in the classroom (particularly her ideas on anger and racism), the racial events beginning in 2012 and continuing into 2021 (as white protestors stormed the US Capitol waving Confederate flags and wearing clothing with racist and anti-Semitic messages) were leading me into despair. It was beginning to feel like the more things change, the more things stay the same. I was tired of the repeated cycle of white supremacy and the persistent controversy over anger in response to it.

The narrative we like to perpetuate as Americans is a story of progress. It goes like this: America had enslaved Africans, but things gradually got better with Reconstruction, the Civil Rights and Voting Rights Acts of the 1960s, the rise of the Black middle class in the 1980s, Obama, and Kamala Harris. This narrative, writes Yale psychologist Jennifer A. Richeson, is a mythology of racial progress. While narratives help us find meaning and order, a myth that tells us that Black American lives have greatly improved *in all areas* distorts reality, promotes victim blaming, and absolves us of responsibility.[5] For if Black lives had improved *in all areas*, why was I, a Black woman, still writing about racism, police brutality, and anger in the twenty-first century? Different decade, same problems. *Will this ever end?* I thought to myself.

However, Lorde's life and work encouraged me. During her own life she kept pushing, living, and working despite discrimination, professional setbacks, and cancer. Even though it was difficult, Lorde learned to use her anger as a transforming force. And so she became an exemplar for me. I too had to learn to keep pushing despite the cycle. I had to learn how to make sense of the rage that I and many others were feeling in response to racism.

Despite the resilience of racism, Lorde's words in "A Litany for Survival" are comforting and challenging:

> Seeking a now that can breed
> futures . . .
> the heavy-footed hoped to silence us . . .
> so it is better to speak
> remembering
> we were never meant to survive[6]

People of color were never meant to survive in a world of white supremacy. But over these last few years as I've witnessed mass protests, listened to the hopes of my young students, and kept my ear to the lips of wise elders, I've observed the miraculous. Here they were, still living, seeking better futures, and refusing to allow the hopes of the heavy-footed to silence their demands for racial justice and their expressions of anger. These facts were powerful enough to hold back the despair.

"But when will this rage end?" asks the interlocutor who tends to diagnose anger as a distinct Western emotion tied to an obsession with individualism and violence. Yes, racism is bad, they admit, but anger and its violent tendency are just as bad, as well as frightening. Lorde addresses this fear at the end of "Uses of Anger." She notes that our fear (or at least our high level of fear) is misdirected. She believes that people have *more reason* to be afraid of the cause of the anger (racism) than the anger itself. She engages in a comparative litany of sorts to remind us that "It is not the anger of Black women which is dripping down over this globe like a diseased liquid. . . . It is not my anger that launches rockets, . . . slaughters children in cities, stockpiles nerve gas and chemical bombs. . . . It is not the anger of Black women which corrodes into blind, dehumanizing power, bent upon the annihilation of us."[7]

James Baldwin was asked a similar question in a 1968 *Esquire* interview. "How can we get the Black people to cool it?" asked th journalist. "It is not for us to cool it," replied Baldwin.[8] Lorde and Baldwin inspire us to ask a different question. Instead of asking when the rage will end, we should ask instead, "When will racism end?" I do not know the answer to this question. Perhaps this is a question that only white folk can ask themselves, since those who practice racism, at least for Toni Morrison, have a "profound neurosis . . . are bereft [and thus] have a very, very serious problem" that only they are in a position to figure out.[9] Maybe racism may never completely end, given this neurosis. But I believe that *its manifestations* in policy, education, health, violence, criminal justice, and day-to-day encounters can decrease. A more just and equitable world is possible. But we will not reach this goal through some form of American determinism, an intoxicating mythology, or a constant fear of our feelings. It requires human effort: a constant struggle against racism.

One thing I know for sure is that if anti-racist anger is in response to racism, and racism is resilient, then the rage must be just as resilient as the racism to combat it. The way that anger remains resilient is by playing the role that I've described in this book. Here is a recap of the role of anger in anti-racist struggle:

- It communicates the value of lives, particularly the racially marginalized and oppressed.
- It alarms us to racism and racial injustice in its explicit and subtle forms.
- It advertises racial justice's worth.
- It makes us believe we can change things.
- It makes us want to take risks to impact the future.
- It makes us optimistic that we can make a less racist and more just world possible.
- It motivates us to engage in productive action to end racial injustice.
- It allows us to resist racial rules that says that only whites have a right to assert their value and receive respect.
- It allows us to resist racial rules that declares that whiteness and white supremacy should be the norm.
- It turns "allies" into rage renegades.

Like a coachable superstar athlete, anti-racist anger can be managed and cultivated to perform these functions at the highest level. Here are some things I've suggested to prevent a person's power through rage from becoming corrupt.

- Get in solidarity with others.
- Express the anger.
- Create goals and plans to achieve racial justice.
- Resist those who will try to silence and dismiss appropriate anti-racist anger.
- Be careful not to use anger to engage in the same supremacy that you are fighting against.

You don't need to cool it first in order to engage in the anti-racist struggle. Because anti-racist anger (what I have referred to as Lordean rage) is aimed at radical change, has an inclusive perspective, motivates productive action, and is also compatible with and complementary to care, compassion, empathy, and love, those who are angry needn't become more respectable or palatable to others in order to engage productively in the struggle. They already have what they need to use their power.

Notes

Preface

1. Picheta (2020).
2. Parker, "LeBron James "Devastated, Hurt, Sad, Mad" Over Breonna Taylor Case Outcome."
3. Harkinson (2016).
4. Du Bois, "Souls of Black Folk," in *Writings*, 359.
5. Washington, "Atlanta Compromise," 585.
6. Cherry, "Anger Can Build a Better World."
7. Myisha Cherry [myishacherry], August 25, 2020, Twitter, https://twitter.com/myishacherry/status/1298302214809632770, and The Atlantic, August 25, 2020, Twitter, https://twitter.com/TheAtlantic/status/1298315141893718019.

Introduction

1. Note the irony: Racism is never rational.
2. Solomon, *Passions*, ix.
3. Nussbaum, *Political Emotions*, 21.
4. Ioanide, *Emotional Politics of Racism*, 6.
5. Jasper, *Emotions of Protest*, 34.
6. Nussbaum, *Anger and Forgiveness*, 39.
7. Ibid., 245.
8. Flanagan, *Geography of Morals*, 205.
9. In the words of Lebron, *Making of Black Lives Matter*, xiv.
10. Norlock refers to this as the "praxis-centered imperfectionist ethic" in "Perpetual Struggle," 6–19.
11. As Candice Delmas describes it. See Delmas (2018).

Chapter 1

1. Seneca, "Of Anger," III.I.
2. From Haidt (2003) citing information from Izard (1977).
3. Nussbaum, *Anger and Forgiveness*, 39.

4. Ibid.
5. This is not to say that the philosophers have only one way of distinguishing anger. Rather, I am highlighting the particular distinctions they make that are relevant to evaluating the anger.
6. Bommarito, "Virtuous and Vicious Anger," 11.
7. Although Owen Flanagan distinguishes anger types by object, intent, feel, etc., I read him as suggesting that—more than not—the anger type's intent is what makes it moral or not.
8. Flanagan, *Geography of Morals*, 205.
9. Butler, *Fifteen Sermons*.
10. Nussbaum, *Anger and Forgiveness*.
11. We can make a distinction between targets as being "*at* whom it is targeted" and "*to* whom it is targeted." A person's anger can be targeted *at* the government if she believes the government is the cause of her anger. But the anger can also be targeted toward or expressed *to* a citizen. By target here, I am referring to targeted *at*. This is not to say that *at* and *to* will not be directed at the same person.
12. Christian Picciolini would later go on to become the author of *Breaking Hate* and help disengage others from hate groups through his nonprofit organization.
13. West, "Hope and Despair," 326.
14. West, *Race Matters*.
15. See Lorde (2007) and Baldwin (1998a).
16. My account of ressentiment rage is a variation influenced by Frantz Fanon's and Friedrich Nietzsche's accounts of anger and what they call "ressentiment." It must be noted, if only briefly, that Nietzsche's account of ressentiment is concerned with providing an account of Christian morality (he calls it slave morality) while Fanon's account is concerned with describing what he sees as colonial projection by the colonized subject. See Fanon (2008) and Nietzsche (1998) for more.
17. West, *Race Matters*.
18. Darby, "White Man Caught on Tape."
19. Hooks, *Killing Rage*, 27.
20. Ibid., 29.
21. Lorde, *Uses of Anger*, 278.
22. McRae, *Anger and the Oppressed*, 114.
23. Ibid., 119.
24. MacRae argues that in the Buddhist tradition, transformative anger is accomplished through contemplative and meditative practices, plus lots of public stories, statues, and rituals.
25. Lorde, *Uses of Anger*, 280.
26. Ibid., 285.
27. Ibid., 284–85.

28. For this reason, Lisa Tessman (2005) refers to the anger of activists as a "burdened virtue."
29. Lorde, *Sister Outsider,* 133.
30. This is Macalester Bell's suggestion in *Hard Feelings.*

Chapter 2

1. "Yale University," Data USA, https://datausa.io/profile/university/yale-university.
2. For a more detailed description of the problems at Yale, see Lewis (2015) and Tan (2015).
3. BBC, "Missouri Race Protests."
4. Woodhouse, "Activists Oust Two Leaders."
5. Hartocollis, "Long after Protests."
6. Madhani and Yu, "Missouri Controversy."
7. An example includes Gilman (2015).
8. Among them are de Sousa (1987) and Moran (1994).
9. D'Arms and Jacobson, "Moralistic Fallacy," 67.
10. To read how Black rage, in particular, is appropriate, see Thompson (2017).
11. What about feeling rage in response to fiction and other art? (In philosophy, this question is known as the paradox of fiction, or the paradox of emotional response to fiction.) What if I hear someone say the N-word in a movie? Can you say, well, it didn't really happen (it was only a movie), so there's nothing to be mad at? I do not think so. As a spectator who is playing along with the "truth of the story," it is fitting to get angry at the character for using the word. That anger represents that fictional world. However, it would be unfitting to get angry at the actor. One's anger could also be in response to the use of the word in the script. This would be a case of representing the real world. An example of this kind of anger was targeted at director Quentin Tarantino for what many believed was an overuse of the N-word in the 2012 movie *Django Unchained.*
12. D'Arms and Jacobson, "Moralistic Fallacy," 66, 71.
13. I admit my own lack of creativity with coming up with "-ful" words to match the emotion (unlike the "funny" or "shameful"). There are no clever responses here, only a direct one. Unfortunately, the "rage-able" or "angry-able" didn't make the cut.
14. Lepoutre, "Rage inside the Machine."
15. Lorde, *Sister Outsider,* 132.
16. See van Prooijen, Douglas, and De Inocencio (2018) for more on emotions and conspiracy theories.
17. Like Mills (2007) claims, the "white" here need not imply that only white people would have white ignorance, nor does every white person have it.
    Mills (2007).

19. Ibid., 35.
20. Mills considers what I call "white skepticism" as part and parcel of white ignorance. I separate the concepts.
21. This is not to say that those with ignorance also by definition have white empathy. All three obstacles are connected, so it is not surprising that a person with white ignorance may also have white skepticism. However, this is not necessarily the case.
22. Empathy for a white person is not the problem. The moral problem with white empathy is that the empathy is to the exclusion of Blacks and at their cost.
23. For more on this concept, read Manne (2018) and Manne (2020).
24. Manne, *Down Girl*, 200–210.
25. Even if I grant that Lordean rage is not apt in a particular case, having it might prevent the person from falling into a false consciousness and getting it wrong about racism in general. In that sense, even if it is wrong in a particular case, it could be a kind of shield against being forced into a distorted worldview.
26. Lugones (1995) recognizes that there are two types of anger: first-order anger and second-order anger. The latter does not desire uptake from "the other world" of sense, while first-order anger does. My use of Lordean rage in this particular example is in the first-order sense. I am not implying that all Lordean rage has this goal. I discuss this more in Chapter 4.
27. Fricker, *Epistemic Injustice*, 1.
28. Hassan, "Hate-Crime Violence."
29. Gover, Harper, and Langton, "Anti-Asian Hate."
30. Bhutta et al., "Disparities in Wealth by Race."
31. King and Barrón-López, "Trump's Refusal to Condemn White Supremacists."
32. Arenge, Perry, and Clark, "Poll: 64 Percent."
33. Sue, *Microaggressions in Everyday Life*, 5.
34. Pierce, "Offensive Mechanisms," 265–66.
35. For a more contemporary treatment of microaggressions, see Rina (2020).
36. Seneca, *De Ira* 11.9.
37. See Bommarito (2017).
38. Srinivasan, "Aptness of Anger," 132.
39. Greene (2020).
40. Bonilla-Silva, "Feeling Race," 17.
41. DiAngelo, *White Fragility*, 28.
42. Kauppinen, "Valuing Anger," 45.

Chapter 3

1. Srinivasan's (2017) response to such a distinction is insightful. She argues that we cannot separate the behaving from the being. I agree.
2. Seneca, *Of Anger* I.I.

3. Ibid., I.II.
4. For more on the connection between motivation and resentment in sports, read Cherry (2019a).
5. Butler, *Fifteen Sermons*, VIII.
6. Ibid.
7. Lorde, *Sister Outsider*, 131.
8. Cooper, *Eloquent Rage*, 170.
9. Traister, *Good and Mad*, 209.
10. Ibid., 208.
11. Ibid., 214.
12. See Berkowitz (1989) and Potegal (1979).
13. Harmon-Jones (2003).
14. Frijda, Kuipers, and ter Schure (1989).
15. See Hewig et al. (2004) and Harmon-Jones and Sigelman (2001) for more details.
16. Harmon-Jones (2003).
17. Lerner and Keltner (2001).
18. Ibid.
19. DeSteno et al. (2004).
20. Aristotle, "Rhetoric" in *Works of Aristotle*, 146.
21. Lerner and Keltner (2001).
22. Cherry (2019a).
23. Lorde, "Uses of Anger," 280.
24. Ibid.
25. Truth, "Women's Rights," 299.
26. Quoted in Zackodnik, *We Must Be Up and Doing*, 283.
27. This does not mean that Wells did not struggle with this anger, given the context of when she was living. Her biographer, Paula J. Giddings, discusses Wells's struggle with her rage due to the stigma around anger for middle-class women. In Chapter 5 I discuss rules around feelings for different people, particularly women and other minorities.
28. Schechter, *Ida B. Well-Barnett and American Reform*, 13–14.
29. Lepoutre, "Rage inside the Machine," 408.
30. Oakes, *Radical and the Republican*, 90–93.
31. Douglass, *My Bondage*, 23.
32. Lorde, "Uses of Anger," 278.
33. Cooper (2018).
34. DiAngelo, *White Fragility*, 2.
35. Frye, in *Politics of Reality*, 89.
36. Lugones, "Hard-to-Handle Anger," 111.
37. Ibid.
38. Nussbaum (2016).
    Pettigrove (2012).

40. See Cherry (2019b); Rieder (2013b); and Blake (2013).
41. Blake, "How MLK Became an Angry Black Man."
42. Rieder (2013c).
43. Blake, "How MLK Became an Angry Black Man." For more details see Rieder 2013a and 2013b.
44. King, *Testament of Hope*, 69.
45. King, *Radical King*, 119.
46. Cherry (2018a).
47. Baldwin, *Price of the Ticket*, 9.

Chapter 4

1. King, *Radical King*, 119.
2. Spelman, "Anger and Insubordination," 266–67.
3. Hochschild, *Emotion Work*, 566.
4. Although Hochschild's account is not exhaustive, it does help us understand feeling rules in the general sense.
5. Saturday Night Live (May 1, 2004)
6. Ibid.
7. Jaggar, "Love and Knowledge," 166.
8. Ibid., 165.
9. Kim, "Racial Emotions," 480.
10. Bonilla-Silva (2019).
11. Kim, "Racial Emotions," 487.
12. Ibid.
13. Du Bois, "The Souls of White Folk," in *Writings*, 924.
14. Ibid., 923.
15. Ibid., 924.
16. Hume, *Essays*, 208.
17. Gabriel, "Timeline of Steve King's Racist Remarks."
18. Owen, "Steve King Went to an Iowa Pizza Hut."
19. Du Bois, "The Souls of White Folk," in *Writings*, 924. This is not Du Bois's recommendation but rather his interpretation of the view.
20. Ibid.
21. For a more detailed discussion of how forgiveness is racialized, see Cherry (forthcoming).
22. See Anderson (2019), Haslanger (1995), and Millet (1971).
23. For example, consider "he is being uppity" and "he is too aggressive" as common accusations.
24. For this reason, Leonard Harris (1999; 2002) refers to emotions like indigntion not as a vice but as a "Walkerian virtue," referring to the abolitionist Da

Walker. It is part of a set of insurrectionist character traits that disrupt racist social practices and embolden racially oppressed people to demand and fight for liberation.

25. Aristotle, *Nicomachean Ethics*, 72.

26. Murphy and Hampton (1988); Dillon (1992).

27. Douglass, *Narrative*, 79.

28. Quoted in ibid., 130.

29. I am inspired here by Kate Manne's (2018) analysis of misogyny. Misogyny, for Manne, is the enforcement wing of patriarchy.

30. For more info on walking while trans, see https://www.thecut.com/2020/07/walking-while-trans-law-in-new-york-explained.html.

31. Rankine, *Citizen*, 30.

32. Audio transcripts obtained by KXAN-TV of Austin available at https://www.kxan.com/news/investigations/trooper-fired-for-sandra-bland-arrest-my-safety-was-in-jeopardy/1052813612 (accessed April 2019).

33. Hill, "Brett Kavanaugh Expressed 'Real Anger' During Testimony."

34. Crenshaw, "We Still Haven't Learned from Anita Hill's Testimony."

35. We can contrast this with police encounters of Black elites and college-educated men, as well as the public's judgment of their anger in these moments. See Tapper, Travers, and Kinan (2009) for more information on Henry Louis Gates's beer summit situation and Crosby (2018) for information on a police encounter with a Black Northwestern University PhD student.

36. Du Bois, "The Souls of White Folk," in *Writings*, 925.

37. In the words of *New Yorker* staff writer Doreen St. Félix (2018), "More than presenting a convincing rebuttal to Ford's extremely credible account, Kavanaugh . . . seemed to be exterminating, live, for an American audience, the faint notion that a massively successful white man could have his birthright questioned or his character held to the most basic type of scrutiny."

38. Thanks to Alice MacLachlan for helping me see this point more clearly.

39. I am sympathetic to the fact that in the case of Obama, as well as in the case of plantation slaves (although quite different contexts), different situations call for different strategies for expressing anger. The consequences can be so great that it would be wise to be strategic with when, how, and to whom a person expresses Lordean rage. But just because strategies differ and people's rage is private doesn't mean that the outraged are not breaking racial rules through rage.

Chapter 5

1. Portland's Black community is only 6 percent of the population. Oregon's Black community is only 2.2 percent.

2. Portland is not the exception. There were overwhelming white crowds in cities across the United States. See Harmon and Tavernise, "One Big Difference."
3. Selsky, "USNA Graduate."
4. Ivy [McKinnon] and Cherry, "Rachel McKinnon on Allies," 136. For her full thoughts read Ivy [McKinnon] (2017).
5. I think a focus on allyship can also fill in some gaps in the allyship and race literature in two ways. First, critics of allyship primarily focus on behaviors and attitudes. They are concerned with the ways in which allies speak, for example, or use their identity as an ally to protect themselves against criticism. This is not to say that behaviors and attitudes will leave the picture. It is only to say that I focus here on the ways in which behaviors and attitudes influence emotions and vice versa. Second, although Janine Young Kim and Eduardo Bonilla-Silva theorize the racial asymmetry of emotions and emotions that arise in the context of race, respectively, I do not think these analyses provide the full extent to which we can examine emotions and race.
6. Gay, "Charge to Be Fair."
7. Although I use the term "ally," I do not mean to ignore these worries about its usage. I use "ally" interchangeably with "rage renegades" to refer to members of a racially dominant group who also have Lordean rage, but this is not to say that the debate concerning its usage shouldn't continue. Words matter.
8. Utt, "Things Allies Need to Know."
9. Ramsey, "Five Tips for Being an Ally."
10. Ivy [McKinnon] (2017) and Cherry (2019b).
11. Mizock and Page (2016).
12. Smith, "Case against Allies."
13. See Harden (2020) and Monroe (2020).
14. Ganesh (2020).
15. See Gilligan (1991), Narayan (1988), and Bell (2009).
16. Jaggar, "Love and Knowledge," 167.
17. Specifically, see Chapters 2 and 4.
18. Bonilla-Silva (2019).
19. See Taylor (2016), particularly his concluding chapter, "It Sucks That I Robbed You; Or, Ambivalence, Appropriation, Joy, and Pain," for more on the ethics of appropriation.
20. Smith (2013).
21. Tosi and Warmke (2020).
22. See Ivy [McKinnon] (2017) and Smith (2013).
23. Ivy points out that allies are often insensitive to constructive criticism and react negatively to it. Here I point to possible reasons why rage renegades could be resistant to criticism.
24. For more on allies blocking criticisms in this way, see Ivy [McKinnon], "Allies Behaving Badly," 172.
25. See Foucault (2003) and Cherry (2017).

26. Ivy [McKinnon] and Cherry, "Rachel McKinnon on Allies," 133–34.

27. Eadens (2020).

28. Novelist Teju Cole's (2020) account of white saviorism has greatly informed my own here.

29. Ibid.

Chapter 6

1. The segment also offered an "anger cleanse" to viewers. See https://www.doctoroz.com/article/anger-detox-plan.

2. For a more extensive treatment on anger management in antiquity see Harris (2001).

3. Seneca, *De Ira* iii.36.1.

4. Ibid., iii.9.

5. See, e.g., Novaco (1975).

6. Kemp and Strongman (1995) offer an extensive analysis of anger management, including Navoco's methods.

7. Nicholson refers to the group as "fury fighters" earlier in the scene.

8. American Psychological Association (2005).

9. Quoted in Mauss (2005).

10. Seneca, *De Ira* ii.

11. Fennell, Benau, and Atchley (2016).

12. Seneca, *De Ira* iii.13.

13. Cherry, "Errors and Limitations of Our 'Anger-Evaluating' Ways," 51.

14. Campbell, "Being Dismissed," 49.

15. Public Enemy, "Fight the Power."

16. Hill, "Black Rage."

17. Lorde, "Uses of Anger," in *Sister Outsider*, 130.

18. Lorde, *Sister Outsider*, 42.

19. Cote (2005).

20. Pennebaker (1997).

21. Lorde, *Sister Outsider*, 41.

22. Baldwin, "A Talk to Teachers," in *Baldwin: Collected Essays*, 681.

23. Baldwin, "Autobiographical Notes," in *Baldwin: Collected Essays*, 5–9.

24. Lorde, *Sister Outsider*, 127.

25. Studies have shown that we are more likely motivated by desire than anger as it pertains to aggression and violence. See McCullough (2008) for more on the seeking system, rage circuit, and aggression.

26. I say "small percentage" here because 93 percent of the protests in 2020 were peaceful, even though the violent ones received lots of media attention. For more information, see Mansoor (2020).

27. Vohs et al. (2011).
28. King, "Other America."
29. King, "Letter from a Birmingham Jail," in *Testament of Hope*, 297.
30. Ibid.
31. Delmas (2018).
32. Lorde, *Sister Outsider*, 127.
33. In this way, the solidarity technique may sound similar to a technique that Roman philosopher Galen of Pergamon once suggested. In his essay *On the Diagnosis and Care of the Passions of the Soul*, Galen describes the role of a moral critic. The critic is wise and is supposed to point out when you are angry. You are to check in with him constantly to see if he detects anger in you. The correction he gives you will free you from anger's harmful effects. However, Galen's technique is quite different from the solidarity technique in several ways.
34. Cherry (2018a).
35. Friedman et al. (2010).
36. Ford, "Protest Fatigue," 164.
37. For more on this see Gorski (2019); Gorski and Chen (2015); and Bunnage (2014).
38. Cherry (2020b).
39. See Locke and Latham (1991). This is not to suggest that goal setting always increases motivation. Goal setting can be less effective under certain conditions, such as when the goals are too ambitious and too many. See also Schroeder and Fishbach (2015).
40. Lorde, *Sister Outsider*, 127. Emphasis added.
41. I recognize that "vision" is an able-bodied person's metaphor. Here I am relying on Lorde's construction.
42. Lorde, *Sister Outsider*, 127.
43. I write in more detail about the anger police in Cherry (2018a) and Cherry (2018b).
44. Lorde, *Sister Outsider*, 127.
45. For more on how women and girls experience this temptation, see Cherry (2020a).
46. Lorde, "Uses of Anger" in *Sister Outsider*, 132.
47. See Stern (2007). The effect looks like the following. You start to see things from the dismissers' point of view. "Maybe I am just bitter," you say. You will wish the dismisser were right, knowing deep down inside that they aren't, and this makes you unsure of what you feel and what you know. However, preventing this gaslight effect is possible.
48. Campbell, "Being Dismissed," 52.
49. Langton (2017).
50. The four anger management techniques we have seen can apply to interpersonal contexts, in addition to the political contexts we associate with Lordean rage.

Chapter 7

1. De Veaux, *Warrior Poet*, 159.
2. Lorde, "Power," in *Selected Works*, 259–60.
3. See De Veaux, *Warrior Poet*, 202.
4. Review of *Sister Outsider* in *Publishers Weekly* 225 (May 25, 1984), 58.
5. Richeson, "Mythology of Racial Progress," 9–12.
6. Lorde, "A Litany for Survival," in *Selected Works*, 283–84.
7. Lorde, "Uses of Anger," in *Sister Outsider*, 133.
8. Esquire, "James Baldwin."
9. Charlie Rose (1993).

Bibliography

Aarts, Henk, Kirsten Ruys, Harm Vieling, Robert Renes, Jasper H. B. de Groot, Anna
M. van Nunen, and Sarit Geertjes. "The Art of Anger: Reward Context Turns
Avoidance Responses to Anger-Related Objects into Approach." *Psychological
Science* 21, no. 10 (2010): 1406–10.

American Psychological Association. *Controlling Anger before It Controls You*. 2005,
https://www.apa.org/topics/anger/control.

Anderson, Elizabeth. "Feminist Epistemology and Philosophy of Science." In
The Stanford Encyclopedia of Philosophy (Summer 2019 Edition), Edward N.
Zalta, ed., https://plato.stanford.edu/archives/sum2019/entries/feminism-
epistemology/.

Arenge, Andrew, Stephanie Perry, and Dartunorro Clark. "Poll: 64 Percent
of Americans Say Racism Remains a Major Problem." NBC, May 29, 2018,
https://www.nbcnews.com/politics/politics-news/poll-64-percent-americans-
say-racism-remains-major-problem-n877536.

Aristotle. *The Works of Aristotle*. Edited by W. D. Ross. Oxford: Clarendon
Press, 1931.

———. *Nicomachean Ethics (Cambridge Texts in the History of Philosophy) 2nd
Edition*. Translated by Roger Crisp. Cambridge, UK: Cambridge University
Press, 2014.

Baldwin, James. *Collected Essays*. New York: Library of America, 1998a.

———. *The Price of the Ticket*. New York: St. Martin's Press, 1998b.

BBC. "Missouri Race Protests: Why Was the University President Forced Out?"
BBC.com, November 9, 2015, https://www.bbc.com/news/world-us-canada-
34772080.

Bell, Macalester. "Anger, Virtue, and Oppression." In *Feminist Ethics and Social
and Political Philosophy: Theorizing the Non-Ideal*, ed. Lisa Tessman, 165–83.
New York: Springer, 2009.

———. *Hard Feelings: The Moral Psychology of Contempt*. New York: Oxford
University Press, 2013.

Berkowitz, Leonard. "Frustration-Aggression Hypothesis: Examination and
Reformulation." *Psychological Bulletin* 106, no. 1 (1989): 59–73.

Bhutta, Neil, Andrew C. Chang, Lisa J. Dettling, and Joanne W. Hsu. "Disparities in
Wealth by Race and Ethnicity in the 2019 Survey of Consumer Finances." *FEDS
Notes*. Washington, DC: Board of Governors of the Federal Reserve System,
September 28, 2020, https://doi.org/10.17016/2380-7172.2797.

Blake, John. "How MLK Became an Angry Black Man." CNN.com, April 16. 2013.

Bommarito, Nicolas. "Virtuous and Vicious Anger." *Journal of Ethics and Social Philosophy* 11, no. 3 (June 2017): 1–28.

Bonilla-Silva, E. "Feeling Race: Theorizing the Racial Economy of Emotions." *American Sociological Review* 84, no. 1 (2019): 1–25.

———. *Racism without Racists: Color-Blind Racism and the Persistence of Racial Inequality in America*. Fifth edition. Lanham, MD: Rowman and Littlefield, 2018.

Bunnage, Leslie. "Social Movement Engagement over the Long Haul: Understanding Activist Retention." *Sociology Compass* 8 (April 2014): 433–45.

Butler, Joseph. *Fifteen Sermons Preached at Rolls Chapel*. Cambridge: Hillard and Brown, 1927, http://anglicanhistory.org/butler/rolls/.

Campbell, Sue. "Being Dismissed: The Politics of Emotional Expression." *Hypatia* 9, no. 3 (Summer 1994): 46–65.

Cherry, Myisha. "State Racism, State Violence, and Vulnerable Solidarity." In *The Oxford Handbook of Philosophy of Race*, ed. Naomi Zack, 352-62. New York: Oxford University Press, 2017.

———. "The Errors and Limitations of Our 'Anger-Evaluating' Ways." In *The Moral Psychology of Anger*, ed. Myisha Cherry and Owen Flanagan, 49–65. Lanham, MD: Rowman and Littlefield, 2018a.

———. "Power Scripts." *New Philosopher Magazine* (Fall 2018b): 62–64.

———. "The Interplay between Resentment, Motivation, and Performance." *Journal of the Philosophy of Sport* 46, no. 2 (Spring 2019a): 147–61.

———. "Love, Anger, and Racial Justice." In *The Routledge Handbook of Love in Philosophy*, ed. Adrienne Martin, 62–64. New York: Routledge, 2019b.

———. "Anger: Embracing the Medusa Trope as a Form of Resistance." In *Philosophy for Girls*, ed. Melissa Shew and Kimberly Garchar, 219–31. (New York: Oxford University Press, 2020a).

———. "Solidarity Care: How to Take Care of Each Other in Times of Struggle." *Public Philosophy Journal* 3, no. 1 (Spring 2020b): https://doi.org/10.25335/PPJ.3.1-4.

———. "Anger Can Build a Better World." *The Atlantic*, August 25, 2020, https://www.theatlantic.com/ideas/archive/2020/08/how-anger-can-build-better-world/615625/.

———. "Racialized Forgiveness." *Hypatia: A Journal of Feminist Philosophy* (forthcoming).

Cole, Teju. "The White Savior Industrial Complex." *The Atlantic*, March 21, 2012, http://www.theatlantic.com/international/archive/2012/03/the-white-savior-industrialcomplex/254843/2/.

Cooper, Brittney. *Eloquent Rage*. New York: St. Martin's Press, 2018.

Cote, Stephane. "A Social Interaction Model of the Effects of Emotion Regulation on Work Strain." *Academy of Management Review* 30, no. 3 (Summer 2005): 509–30.

Crenshaw, Kimberle. "We Still Haven't Learned from Anita Hill's Testimony." *New York Times*, September 27, 2018, https://www.nytimes.com/2018/09/27/opinion/anita-hill-clarence-thomas-brett-kavanaugh-christine-ford.html.

Crosby, Lawrence. "Police Tackled Me for Stealing a Car. It Was My Own." *Chicago Tribune*, July 3, 2018, https://www.chicagotribune.com/news/opinion

commentary/ct-perspec-police-evanston-racial-profiling-black-man-0704-story.html.

Darby, Luke. "White Man Caught on Tape Screaming at Airport Police for 'Treating Me Like a F*cking Black Person.'" *GQ Magazine*, August 18, 2018, https://www.gq.com/story/white-man-airport-treating-me-black-person?verso=true.

D'Arms, Justin, and Daniel Jacobson. "The Moralistic Fallacy: On the 'Appropriateness' of Emotions." *Philosophy and Phenomenological Research* 61, no. 1 (July 2000): 65–90.

Delmas, Candice. *A Duty to Resist: When Disobedience Should Be Uncivil.* New York: Oxford University Press, 2018.

De Sousa, Ronald. *The Rationality of Emotion.* Boston: MIT Press, 1987.

DeSteno, David, Richard E. Petty, Derek D. Rucker, Duane T. Wegener, and Julia Braverman. "Discrete Emotions and Persuasion: The Role of Emotion-Induced Expectancies." *Journal of Personality and Social Psychology* 86, no. 1 (February 2004): 43–56.

De Veaux, Alexis. *Warrior Poet: A Biography of Audre Lorde.* New York: Norton, 2004.

DiAngelo, Robin. *White Fragility.* Boston: Beacon Press, 2018.

Dillon, Robin. "Toward a Feminist Conception of Self-Respect." *Hypatia: A Journal of Feminist Philosophy* 7, no. 1 (1992): 52–69.

Douglass, Frederick. *My Bondage, My Freedom.* Maryland: Start Publishing LLC, 2013.

———. *Narrative of the Life of Frederick Douglass, An American Slave, Written by Himself.* Ed. William L. Andrews and William S. McFeeling. New York: Norton Critical Edition, 1997.

Du Bois, W. E. B. *Writings.* Ed. Nathan Huggins. New York: Library of America, 1986.

Eadens, Savannah. "Viral Photo Shows Line of White People between Police, Black Protesters at Thursday Rally." *Louisville Courier Journal*, May 29, 2020, https://www.courier-journal.com/story/news/local/2020/05/29/breonna-taylor-photo-white-women-between-police-black-protesters/5286416002/.

Esquire. "James Baldwin: How to Cool It." *Esquire*, April 2, 2017, https://www.esquire.com/news-politics/a23960/james-baldwin-cool-it/.

Fanon, Frantz. *Black Skin, White Masks.* New York: Grove Press, 2008.

Fennell, Alexander B., Erik Benau, and Ruth Ann Atchley. "A Single Session of Meditation Reduces Physiological Indices of Anger in Both Experienced and Novice Meditators." *Consciousness and Cognition* 40 (2016): 54–66.

Flanagan, Owen. *The Geography of Morals: Varieties of Moral Possibility.* New York: Oxford University Press, 2016.

Fontaine, Johnny, Klaus R. Scherer, Etienne B. Roesch, and Phoebe C. Ellsworth. "Emotion Is for Doing: The Action Tendency Component1." In *Components of Emotional Meaning*, ed. Johnny J. R. Fontaine, Klaus R. Scherer, and Cristina Soriano, 170–85. Oxford: Oxford University Press, 2013.

Ford, Richard Thompson. "Protest Fatigue." In *Protest and Dissent*, ed. Melissa Schwartzberg, Nomos LXII, 161–88. New York: New York University Press, 2020.

Foucault, Michel. *Society Must Be Defended. Lectures at the Collège de France, 1975–1976 (No. 3).* New York: Picador, 2003.

French, Peter. "Virtuous Avengers in Commonplace Cases." *Philosophia* 44 (June 2016): 381–93.

Fricker, Miranda. *Epistemic Injustice: Power and the Ethics of Knowing.* New York: Oxford University Press, 2007.

Friedman, Ron, Edward L. Deci, Andrew J. Elliot, and Arlen C. Molleret. "Motivational Synchronicity: Priming Motivational Orientations with Observations of Others' Behaviors." *Motivation and Emotion* 34, no. 1 (March 2010): 34–38.

Frijda, Nico H. *The Emotions.* Cambridge: Cambridge University Press, 1986.

———. "Emotion, Cognitive Structure, and Action Tendency." *Cognition and Emotion* 1, no. 2 (1987): 115–43.

Frijda, Nico, Peter Kuipers, and Elisabeth ter Schure. "Relations among Emotion, Appraisal, and Emotional Action Readiness." *Journal of Personality and Social Psychology* 57, no. 2 (1989): 212–28.

Frye, Marilyn. *The Politics of Reality: Essays in Feminist Theory.* Berkeley, CA: Crossing Press, 1983.

Gabriel, Trip. "A Timeline of Steve King's Racist Remarks and Divisive Actions." *New York Times*, January 15, 2019, https://www.nytimes.com/2019/01/15/us/politics/steve-king-offensive-quotes.html.

Galen. *On the Diagnosis and Care of the Passions of the Soul*, Ed. Paul W. Harkins. Athens, Ohio: Ohio University Press, 1964.

Ganesh, Chandni. "A Fearless Woman Protested Naked in Portland. Then She Was Shot At." *Upworthy*, July 22, 2020, https://scoop.upworthy.com/a-white-passing-woman-protested-naked-in-portland-she-was-still-shot-at.

Garza, Alicia. "Ally or Co-conspirator?: What It Means to Act #InSolidarity." *Movetoendviolence.org*, 2016.

Gay, Roxane. "The Charge to Be Fair: Ta-Nehisi Coates and Roxane Gay in Conversation." *Barnes and Noble*, August 10, 2015, https://www.barnesandnoble.com/review/the-charge-to-be-fair-ta-nehisi-coates-and-roxane-gay-in-conversation.

Gilligan, Carol. "Joining the Resistance: Psychology, Politics, Girls and Women." In *The Female Body: Figures, Styles, Speculations*, ed. Laurence Goldstein, 12–47. Ann Arbor: University of Michigan Press, 1991.

Gilman, Ollie. "The Moment Yale Students Encircled and Shouted Down Professor Who Told Them to Just 'Look Away' If They Were Offended by Halloween Costumes." *Daily Mail*, November 7, 2015, https://www.dailymail.co.uk/news/article-3308422/Students-rage-professor-sent-email-telling-students-just-look-away-offended-Halloween-costumes.html.

Gorski, Paul C. "Racial Battle Fatigue and Activist Burnout in Racial Justice Activists of Color at Predominately White Colleges and Universities." *Race, Ethnicity, and Education* 22, no. 1 (2019): 1–20.

Gorski, Paul C., and C. Chen. "Burnout in Social Justice and Human Rights Activists: Symptoms, Causes, and Implications." *Journal of Human Rights Practice* 7 (2015): 366–90.

Gover, Angela, Shannon Harper, and Lynn Langton. "Anti-Asian Hate Crime during the COVID-19 Pandemic: Exploring the Reproduction of Inequality." *American Journal of Criminal Justice* 45 (July 2020): 647–67.

Greene, Stacey. "Are We There Yet? Perceptions of Racial Progress among Racial Minorities." *PS: Political Science & Politics* 53, no. 4 (2020): 685–89.

Greenfieldboyce, Nell. "The Power of Martin Luther King Jr.'s Anger." NPR, February 20, 2019, https://www.npr.org/sections/codeswitch/2019/02/20/691298594/the-power-of-martin-luther-king-jr-s-anger.

Haidt, Jonathan. "The Moral Emotions." In *Handbook of Affective Sciences,* ed. R. J. Davidson, K. R. Scherer, and H. H. Goldsmith, 852–70. Oxford: Oxford University Press, 2003.

Harden, Kevin. "Wall of Moms Leader Ousted after Clash." *Portland Tribune*, August 1, 2020, https://pamplinmedia.com/pt/9-news/475587-384413-wall-of-moms-leader-ousted-after-clash?.

Harkinson, Josh. "Meet the White Nationalist Trying to Ride the Trump Train to Lasting Power." *Mother Jones,* October 2016, https://www.motherjones.com/politics/2016/10/richard-spencer-trump-alt-right-white-nationalist/.

Harmon, Amy, and Tavernise, Sabrina. "One Big Difference about George Floyd Protests: Many White Faces." *New York Times*, June 17, 2020, https://www.nytimes.com/2020/06/12/us/george-floyd-white-protesters.html.

Harmon-Jones, Eddie. "Anger and the Behavioral Approach System." *Personality and Individual Differences* 35 (2003): 995–1005.

——. "Clarifying the Emotive Functions of Asymmetrical Frontal Cortical Activity." *Psychophysiology* 40, no. 6 (September 2003): 838–48.

Harmon-Jones, Eddie, and J. Sigelman. "State Anger and Prefrontal Brain Activity: Evidence That Insult-Related Relative Left-Prefrontal Activation Is Associated with Experienced Anger and Aggression." *Journal of Personality & Social Psychology* 80, no. 5 (2001): 797–803.

Harris, Leonard. "Honor and Insurrection or A Short Story about Why John Brown (with David Walker's Spirit) Was Right and Frederick Douglass (with Benjamin Banneker's Spirit) Was Wrong." In *Frederick Douglass: A Critical Reader*, ed. Bill Lawson and Frank Kirkland, 227–42. Malden, MA: Blackwell, 1999.

——. "Insurrectionist Ethics: Advocacy, Moral Psychology, and Pragmaticism." In *Ethical Issues for a New Millennium*, ed. John Howie, 192–210. Carbondale: Southern Illinois University Press, 2002.

Harris, William V. *Restraining Rage: The Ideology of Anger Control in Classical Antiquity*. Cambridge, MA: Harvard University Press, 2001.

Hartocollis, Anemona. "Long after Protests, Students Shun the University of Missouri." *New York Times*, July 9, 2017, https://www.nytimes.com/2017/07/09/us/university-of-missouri-enrollment-protests-fallout.html.

Haslanger, Sally. "Ontology and Social Construction." *Philosophical Topics 23*, no 2 (1995): 95–125.

Hassan, Adel. "Hate-Crime Violence Hits 16-Year High, F.B.I. Reports." *New York Times*, November 12, 2019, https://www.nytimes.com/2019/11/12/us/hate-crimes-fbi-report.html.

Hemmings, Carrie, and Amanda Evans. "Identifying and Treating Race-Based Trauma in Counseling." *Journal of Multicultural Counseling and Development* 46, no. 1 (January 2018): 20–39.

Hewig, Johannes, D. Hagemann, J. Seifert, E. Naumann, and D. Bartussek. "On the Selective Relation of Frontal Cortical Asymmetry and Anger-Out versus Anger-Control." *Journal of Personality and Social Psychology* 87, no. 6 (December 2004): 926–39.

Hill, Anita. "Brett Kavanaugh Expressed 'Real Anger' during Testimony." Associated Press, September 28, 2018, https://www.usatoday.com/story/news/politics/2018/09/28/anita-hill-brett-kavanaugh-testimony-showed-aggression/1456138002/.

Hill, Lauryn. "Black Rage." 2014. https://www.youtube.com/watch?v=l_sdubWaY5o.

Hochschild, Arlie Russell. "Emotion Work, Feeling Rules, and Social Structure." *American Journal of Sociology* 85, no. 3 (November 1979): 551–75.

hooks, bell. *Killing Rage: Ending Racism.* New York: H. Holt and Co., 1995.

Hume, David. *Essays: Moral, Political, and Literary.* Indianapolis: Liberty Fund, 1987.

Ioanide, Paula. *The Emotional Politics of Racism.* Stanford, CA: Stanford University Press, 2015.

Ivy, Veronica (Rachel McKinnon). "Allies Behaving Badly: Gaslighting as Epistemic Injustice." In *Routledge Handbook of Epistemic Injustice*, ed. Ian James Kidd, José Medina, and Gaile Pohlhaus Jr., 167–74. New York: Routledge, 2017.

Ivy, Veronica (Rachel McKinnon), and Myisha Cherry. "Rachel McKinnon on Allies and Ally Culture." In *Unmuted: Conversations on Prejudice, Oppression, and Social Justice*, 57–62. New York: Oxford University Press, 2019.

Izard, Carroll. *Human Emotions.* New York: Plenum Press, 1977.

Jaggar, Alison M. "Love and Knowledge: Emotion in Feminist Epistemology." *Inquiry* 32, no. 2 (1989): 151–76.

Jasper, James. *The Emotions of Protest.* Chicago: University of Chicago Press, 2018.

Kauppinen, Antti. "Valuing Anger." In *The Moral Psychology of Anger*, ed. Myisha Cherry and Owen Flanagan, 31–48. Lanham, MD: Rowman and Littlefield, 2018.

Kemp, Simon, and K. T. Strongman. "Anger Theory and Management: A Historical Analysis." *American Journal of Psychology* 108, no. 3 (Autumn 1995): 397–417.

Kim, Janine Young. "Racial Emotions and the Feeling of Equality." *University of Colorado Law Review* 87 / Chapman University, Fowler Law Research Paper No. 16-11 (March 2016), https://ssrn.com/abstract=2807071.

King, Martin Luther, Jr. "The Other America." 1968, https://www.gphistorical.org/mlk/mlkspeech/.

———. *A Testament of Hope: The Essential Writings and Speeches of Martin Luther King Jr.*, ed. James Melvin Washington. New York: HarperCollins, 1986.

———. *The Radical King.* Ed. Cornel West. Boston: Beacon Press, 2015.

King, Maya, and Laura Barrón-López. "Trump's Refusal to Condemn White Supremacists Launches an Online Furor." *Politico*, September 30, 2020, https://www.politico.com/news/2020/09/30/trump-proud-boys-white-supremacy-423464.

Lebron, Chris. *The Making of Black Lives Matter.* New York: Oxford University Press, 2017.

Langton, Rae. "Virtues of Resentment." *Utilitas* 13, no. 2 (2001): 255–62.

———. "Blocking as Counter-Speech." In *New Work on Speech Acts*, ed. Daniel Harris, Daniel Fogal, and Matt Moss, 144–64. New York: Oxford University Press, 2017.

Late Night with Seth Myers. "White Savior: The Movie Trailer." NBC Broadcasting, February 21, 2019.

Lepoutre, Maxime. "Rage inside the Machine: Defending the Place of Anger in Democratic Speech." *Politics, Philosophy & Economics* 17, no. 4 (November 2018): 398–426.

Lerner, Jennifer, and Dacher Keltner. "Fear, Anger, and Risk." *Journal of Personality and Social Psychology* 81, no. 1 (2001): 146–59.

Lewis, Aaron. "I'm a Yale student, and This School's Problems with Race Go Much Deeper Than Halloween Costumes." *Quartz.com*, 2015, https://qz.com/546403/yale-student-protests/.

Locke, Gary, and Edwin Latham. "A Theory of Goal Setting & Task Performance." *Academy of Management Review* 16, no. 2 (April 1991): 211–47.

Lorde, Audre. "The Uses of Anger." *Women's Studies Quarterly* 1 & 2 (1997): 278–85.

———. *Sister Outsider*. New York: Ten Speed Press, 2007.

———. *The Selected Works of Audre Lorde*. Edited and introduction by Roxane Gay. New York: Norton, 2020.

Lugones, María. "Hard-to-Handle Anger." In *Overcoming Racism and Sexism*, ed. Linda A. Bell and David Blumenfeld, 103–18. Lanham, MD: Rowman and Littlefield, 1995.

MacLachlan, Alice. "Practicing Imperfect Forgiveness." In *Feminist Ethics and Social and Political Philosophy: Theorizing the Non-Ideal*, ed. Lisa Tessman, 185–204. New York: Springer, 2009.

Madhani, Aamer, and Roger Yu. "Missouri Controversy Highlights Academia's Free Speech Struggle." *USA Today*, November 12, 2015, https://www.usatoday.com/story/news/2015/11/12/missouri-yale-campus-speech-first-amendment/75600646/.

Manne, Kate. *Down Girl: The Logic of Misogyny*. New York: Oxford University Press, 2018.

———. *Entitled*. New York: Crown, 2020.

Mansoor, Sanya. "93% of Black Lives Matter Protests Have Been Peaceful, New Report Finds." *Time*, September 5, 2020, https://time.com/5886348/report-peaceful-protests/.

Mauss, Iris. "Control Your Anger!" In *Scientific American Mind* 16, no. 4 (2005): 64–71.

McCullough, Michael E. *Beyond Revenge: The Evolution of the Forgiveness Instinct*. San Francisco: Jossey-Bass, 2008.

McRae, Emily. "Metabolizing Anger: A Tantric Buddhist Solution to the Problem of Moral Anger." *Philosophy East and West* 65, no. 2 (April 2015): 466–84.

———. "Anger and the Oppressed." In *The Moral Psychology of Anger*, ed. Myisha Cherry and Owen Flanagan, 105–22. Lanham, MD: Rowman and Littlefield, 2018.

Michener, Sara. "SJW Behaviors That Hurt Social Justice." Medium.com, 2017, https://medium.com/human-development-project/sjw-behaviors-that-hurt-social-justice-a445916583ce.

Millett, Kate. *Sexual Politics*. London: Granada Publishing, 1971.

Mills, Charles. "White Ignorance." In *Race and Epistemologies of Ignorance*, ed. Shannon Sullivan and Nancy Tuana, 11–38. Albany, NY: SUNY Press, 2007.

Mizock, Lauren, and Konjit Page. "Evaluating the Ally Role." *Journal for Social Action in Counseling and Psychology* 8, no. 1 (Summer 2016): 7–33.

Monroe, Irene. "The White Women of Portland, Oregon Aren't Listening." WGBH, August 5, 2020, https://www.wgbh.org/news/commentary/2020/08/05/the-white-women-of-portland-oregon-arent-listening.

Moran, Richard. "The Expression of Feeling in Imagination." *Philosophical Review* 103, no. 1 (January 1994): 75–106.

Murphy, Jeffrie G., and Jean Hampton. *Forgiveness and Mercy*. New York: Cambridge University Press, 1988.

Narayan, Uma. "Working Together across Differences: Some Considerations on Emotions and Political Practice." *Hypatia: A Journal of Feminist Philosophy* 3, no. 2 (1988): 31–47.

Nietzsche, Friedrich. *On the Genealogy of Morality*. New York: Cambridge University Press, 1998.

Norlock, Kathryn J. "Perpetual Struggle." *Hypatia: A Journal of Feminist Philosophy* 34, no. 1 (Winter 2019): 6–19.

Novaco, Raymond. *Anger Control: The Development and Evaluation of an Experimental Treatment*. Lexington, MA: Lexington Books, 1975.

Nussbaum, Martha C. *Political Emotions*. Cambridge, MA: Harvard University Press, 2013.

———. *Anger and Forgiveness: Resentment, Generosity, Justice*. New York: Oxford University Press, 2016.

———. "From Anger to Love: Self-Purification and Political Resistance." In *To Shape a New World: Essays on the Political Philosophy of Martin Luther King Jr.*, ed. Brandon M. Terry and Tommie Shelby, 105–26. Cambridge, MA: Harvard University Press, 2018.

Oakes, James. *The Radical and the Republican: Frederick Douglass, Abraham Lincoln, and the Triumph of Antislavery Politics*. New York: W. W. Norton, 2008.

Owen, Tess. "Steve King Went to an Iowa Pizza Hut to Declare Western Civilization Superior." *ViceNews*, December 5, 2019, https://www.vice.com/en/article/qvggkw/steve-king-went-to-an-iowa-pizza-hut-to-declare-western-civilization-superior.

Parker, Ryan. "LeBron James Devastated, Hurt, Sad, Mad Over Breonna Taylor Case Outcome." *The Hollywood Reporter*, September 24, 2020, https://www.hollywoodreporter.com/news/general-news/lebron-james-devastated-hurt-sad-mad-over-breonna-taylor-case-outcome-4066401/

Pennebaker, James. *Opening Up: The Healing Power of Expressing Emotions*. New York: Guilford, 1997.

Pettigrove, Glen. "Meekness and 'Moral' Anger." *Ethics* 122, no. 2 (2012): 341–70.

Picheta, Rob. "Now Is the Time: Emotional John Boyega Addresses Protesters at London Black Lives Matter Rally." CNN.com, June 3, 2020, https://www.cnn.

com/2020/06/03/uk/john-boyega-london-floyd-protest-scli-gbr-intl/index.
html.

Pierce, Chester. "Offensive Mechanisms." In *The Black Seventies*, ed. Floyd Barbour, 265–82. Boston: P. Sargent, 1970.

Potegal, Michael. "The Reinforcing Value of Several Types of Aggressive Behavior: A Review." *Aggressive Behavior* 5, no. 4 (October 1979): 353–73.

Public Enemy. "Fight the Power." Motown, 1989.

Publishers Weekly. "Review of Sister Outsider." *Publishers Weekly* 225 (May 25, 1984): 58.

Ramsey, Franchesca. "Five Tips for Being an Ally." YouTube, November 22, 2014, https://youtu.be/_dg86g-QlM0.

Rankine, Claudia. *Citizen: An American Lyric*. Minneapolis: Graywolf Press, 2014.

Richeson, Jennifer A. "The Mythology of Racial Progress." *The Atlantic* 326, no. 2 (September 2020): 9–12.

Rieder, Jonathan. *Gospel of Freedom: Martin Luther King, Jr.'s Letter from Birmingham Jail and the Struggle That Changed a Nation*. New York: Bloomsbury Press, 2013a.

———. "Dr. King's Righteous Fury." *The New York Times*, April 15, 2013b, https://www.nytimes.com/2013/04/16/opinion/dr-kings-righteous-fury.html.

———. "The Day President Kennedy Embraced Civil Rights—and the Story Behind It." *The Atlantic*, June 11, 2013c, https://www.theatlantic.com/national/archive/2013/06/the-day-president-kennedy-embraced-civil-rights-and-the-story-behind-it/276749/.

Rina, Regina. *The Ethics of Microaggression*. New York: Routledge, 2020.

Rose, Charlie. Interview with Toni Morrison. PBS, May 7, 1993. https://charlierose.com/videos/18778.

Saturday Night Live. "Debbie Downer: Disney World." NBC Broadcasting, May 1, 2004.

———. "Debbie Downer: Thanksgiving Dinner." NBC Broadcasting, November 20, 2004.

———. "Debbie Downer: Weding Reception." NBC Broadcasting, October 1, 2005.

———. "Impossible Hulk." NBC Broadcasting, March 9, 2019.

Schechter, Patricia Ann. "All the Intensity of My Nature: Ida B. Wells, Anger, and Politics." *Radical History Review* 70 (Winter 1998): 48–77.

———. *Ida B. Wells-Barnett and American Reform, 1880–1930*. Chapel Hill: University of North Carolina Press, 2001.

Scheiter, Krissana. "Aristotle on the Purpose of Revenge." In *Best Served Cold: Studies on Revenge*, ed. Sheila Bibb and Daniel Escandell Montiel, 3–11. Oxford: Inter-Disciplinary Press, 2010, https://www.researchgate.net/profile/Daniel_Escandell_Montiel/publication/235889887_Best_Served_Cold_Studies_on_Revenge/links/00b7d5350253e1dfd2000000/Best-Served-Cold-Studies-on-Revenge.pdf.

Schroeder, Juliana, and Ayelet Fishbach. "How to Motivate Yourself and Others? Intended and Unintended Consequences." *Research in Organizational Behavior* 35 (2015): 123–41.

Selsky, Andrew. "USNA Graduate, Vet Christopher David Beaten by Federal Agents in Portland: 'They Came Out to Fight.'" CBS Baltimore, July 21, 2020, https://

baltimore.cbslocal.com/2020/07/21/usna-graduate-vet-christopher-david-beaten-by-federal-agents-in-portland/.

Seneca, Lucius. "De Ira." In *Anger, Mercy, Revenge*. Chicago: University of Chicago Press. 2012.

————. "Of Anger: Book I." In *L. Annaeus Seneca, Minor Dialogues Together with the Dialogue "On Clemency."* Translated by Aubrey Steward. London: Bohn's Classical Library Edition, 1900, https://en.wikisource.org/wiki/Of_Anger/Book_I.

Smith, Adam. *Theory of Moral Sentiments*, ed. D.D. Raphael and A.L. Mackie. Oxford, UK: Oxford University Press, 1978.

Smith, Mychal Denzel. "The Case against Allies." Feministing Blog, October 1, 2013. http://feministing.com/2013/10/01/the-case-against-allies/.

Solomon, Robert. *The Passions*. Indianapolis: Hackett Publishing, 1993.

Spelman, Elizabeth. "Anger and Insubordination." In *Women, Knowledge, and Reality: Explorations in Feminist Philosophy*, ed. Ann Garry and Marilyn Pearsall, 263–73. London: Routledge, 1989.

Srinivasan, Amia. "The Aptness of Anger." *Journal of Political Philosophy* 26, no. 2 (June 2017): 123–44.

Stern, Robin. *The Gaslight Effect*. New York: Harmony Books, 2007.

St. Félix, Doreen. "The Ford-Kavanaugh Hearing Will Be Remembered as a Grotesque Display of Patriarchal Resentment." *New Yorker*, September 27, 2018, https://www.newyorker.com/culture/cultural-comment/the-ford-kavanaugh-hearings-will-be-remembered-for-their-grotesque-display-of-patriarchal-resentment.

Straus, Murray, and Richard J. Gelles. *Physical Violence in American Families*. Piscataway, NJ: Transaction Publishers, 1990.

Sue, Derald Wing. *Microaggressions in Everyday Life: Race, Gender, and Sexual Orientation*. Newark, NJ: John Wiley and Sons, 2010.

Sullivan, Shannon, and Nancy Tuana. "Introduction." In *Race and Epistemologies of Ignorance*, ed. Shannon Sullivan and Nancy Tuana, 1–10. Albany, NY: SUNY Press, 2007.

Tan, Avianne. "The Allegations of Racism at Yale That Culminated in Over 1,000 Marching for Justice on Campus." ABC News, November 10, 2015, https://abcnews.go.com/US/allegations-racism-yale-culminated-1000-marching-justice-campus/story?id=35105491.

Tapper, Jake, Karen Travers, and Huma Khan. "Obama, Biden Sit Down for Beers with Gates, Crowley." ABC, July 30, 2009, https://abcnews.go.com/Politics/story?id=8208602&page=1.

Taylor, Paul. *Black Is Beautiful: A Philosophy of Black Aesthetics*. Malden, MA: Wiley Blackwell, 2016.

Tessman, Lisa. *The Burdened Virtues: Virtue Ethics for Liberatory Struggle*. New York: Oxford University Press, 2005.

Thompson, Debra. "An Exoneration of Black Rage." *South Atlantic Quarterly* 116, no. 3 (July 2017): 457–81.

Tosi, Justin, and Brandon Warmke. *Grandstanding*. New York: Oxford University Press, 2020.

Traister, Rebecca. *Good and Mad: The Revolutionary Power of Women's Anger.* New York: Simon and Schuster, 2018.

Truth, Sojourner. "Women's Rights." In *We Must Be Up and Doing: A Reader in Early African American Feminisms*, ed. Teresa C. Zackodnik, 281. Buffalo, NY: Broadview Press, 2010.

Utt, Jaime. "Things Allies Need to Know." Everyday Feminism, November 2013. https://everydayfeminism.com/2013/11/things-allies-need-to-know/.

Van Prooijen, Jan-Willem, Karen Douglas, and Clara De Inocencio. "Connecting the Dots: Illusory Pattern Perception Predicts Belief in Conspiracies and the Supernatural." *European Journal of Social Psychology* 48, no. 3 (April 2018): 320–35.

Vohs, Kathleen D., Brian D. Glass, W. Todd Maddox, and Arthur B. Markman. "Ego Depletion Is Not Just Fatigue: Evidence from a Total Sleep Deprivation Experiment." *Social Psychological and Personality Science* 2, no. 2 (March 2011): 166–73.

Washington, Booker T. "The Manuscript Version of the Atlantic Exposition Speech." In *The Booker T. Washington Papers, Vol. 3*, ed. Louis R. Harlan, 583–87. Chicago: University of Illinois Press, 1974.

West, Cornel. *Race Matters.* Boston: Beacon Press, 1993.

———. "Hope and Despair: Past and Present." In *To Shape a New World: Essays on the Political Philosophy of Martin Luther King Jr.*, ed. Brandon Terry and Tommie Shelby, 325–37. Cambridge, MA: Harvard University Press, 2018.

Woodhouse, Kelly. "Activists Oust Two Leaders." *Inside Higher Education*, November 10, 2015, https://www.insidehighered.com/news/2015/11/10/u-missouri-leaders-resign-amid-student-concerns-over-racism-and-diversity.

Zackodnik, Teresa C. *We Must Be Up and Doing: A Reader in Early African American Feminisms.* Buffalo, NY: Broadview Press, 2010.

Index